"I thoroughly enjoy Barney Ca   ons are terrific."

> —**Francine Rivers**, *New York Times* best-selling author

"Barney Cargile speaks from the heart as he writes, opening up our hearts in the process. He points us back to the Bible using his own incidents, even the painful ones, as testimonies of how God works through him, and now can work through us. He is a great encourager, and his book will bless you."

> —**Jeffrey Daly**, founder and executive director,
> National Day of Repentance

"Barney Cargile's writings present a relevant picture that makes truth come alive."

> —**Bret Avlakeotes**, pastor, Spring Hills Community Church

"Barney Cargile's reflections are delightful and fresh. Nobody I know does it better."

> —**Jeff Johnson**, director, Sonoma County Young Life

"Barney Cargile uses vivid pictures and stories to make spiritual truth come to life. You'll benefit from the insights he provides."

> —**Rick Bassett**, pastor, Santa Rosa Nazarene Church

THE
PERFECT
SAVIOUR

Celebrating
the
Living Hope
of Easter

BARNEY CARGILE III

Our Daily Bread
Publishing.

The Perfect Saviour: Celebrating the Living Hope of Easter
© 2024 by Barney Cargile III

Interior design by Michael J. Williams

ISBN,978-1-916718-44-9

Library of Congress Catalogueueueueueueueueing-in-Publication Data Available

Printed in the United Kingdom
25 26 27 28 29 30 31 32 / 8 7 6 5 4 3 2 1

CONTENTS

Preface: A Life-Altering Story 9
Introduction 11

Part One: The Plan before Time 13

1. Morning: A Preplanned Touchdown 15
  Evening: Working behind the Scenes 17

2. Morning: It's All About You 19
  Evening: Of Matchless Worth 21

3. Morning: Angels Gone Wild 23
  Evening: Judge and Jury 25

4. Morning: Of Flying Refrigerators and Prophecy 27
  Evening: Cheering for All Eternity 29

Part Two: The Journey with Jesus 31

5. Morning: "Who Do You Say I Am?" (Part 1) 33
  Evening: "Who Do You Say I Am?" (Part 2) 35

6. Morning: Jesus Resolutely Set Out 37
  Evening: Holding Your Breath 39

7. Morning: Empty 41
  Evening: "Cinderella, It's Me!" 43

8. Morning: Ministering to the Lost 45
  Evening: Not Allowed to Die 47

9. Morning: A Crying God 49
  Evening: The Little Donkey 51

Part Three: The Night from Hell   53

10.   Morning: So . . .   55
        Evening: The Father's House   57

11.   Morning: "Show Us the Way"   59
        Evening: "Remain in Me"   61

12.   Morning: Garden of the Oil Press   63
        Evening: "Not My Will"   65

13.   Morning: Who's in Charge?   67
        Evening: Sweet Tea   69

14.   Morning: A Faithful Friend   71
        Evening: To This You Were Called   73

15.   Morning: A Cowardly Judge   75
        Evening: Treated Like a Common Criminal   77

Part Four: The Cross   79

16.   Morning: Pure Sacrificial Love   81
        Evening: Excruciating   83

17.   Morning: "Father, Forgive Them"   85
        Evening: "Today You Will Be with Me"   87

18.   Morning: The Personal Nature of the Cross   89
        Evening: "It Is Finished"   91

19.   Morning: Darkness during Daylight   93
        Evening: Access to God's Office   95

20.   Morning: The Headless Snake   97
        Evening: Love Wounds   99

21.   Morning: Do It Yourself   101
        Evening: Eggy-Weggy   103

22.   Morning: Inky's Escape   105
        Evening: Hope in a Gulag   107

23.   Morning: Peace Child   109
        Evening: Saved by a Rubber Ducky   111

24.   Morning: Rare Coins   113
       Evening: Lost   115

Part Five: The Resurrection   117

25.   Morning: The Resurrection on Trial   119
       Evening: Chocolate Bunnies   121

26.   Morning: Life to Death to Life   123
       Evening: The Transforming Power of the Resurrection   125

27.   Morning: "I'll Meet You after the Resurrection"   127
       Evening: The Real Jesus   129

28.   Morning: Hope on the Highway   131
       Evening: Jesus and Sleeping Beauty   133

29.   Morning: "Surprise, I'm Alive!"   135
       Evening: Ice Surfing with Jesus   137

30.   Morning: A Knockout Blow   139
       Evening: The Shadow of Death   141

31.   Morning: Obsessed with Death   143
       Evening: A Living Hope   145

32.   Morning: It's Not Enough   147
       Evening: He Can Do Anything   149

Part Six: The Holy Week   151

33.   Palm Sunday   153
       Morning: When Jesus Came to Town   155
       Evening: Get Off Your High Horse   157

34.   Monday   159
       Morning: A Different Side of Jesus (Part 1)   161
       Evening: A Different Side of Jesus (Part 2)   163

35.   Tuesday   165
       Morning: Fake Fronts   167
       Evening: Radical Generosity   169

36. Wednesday   171
    Morning: Flowers for Jesus   173
    Evening: The Bitterness of Betrayal   175

37. Maundy Thursday   177
    Morning: Bigger Than Us   179
    Evening: Jesus Knows Injustice   181

38. Good Friday   183
    Morning: A Twisted Kiss   185
    Evening: The Shock of the Cross   187

39. Holy Saturday   189
    Morning: The Saddest of Saturdays   191
    Evening: The Beauty of Burial   193

40. Easter Sunday   195
    Morning: Didn't See *That* Coming!   197
    Evening: All Is Well   199

Epilogue: What the Resurrection Means to Me   201
A Final Word   203
About the Author   205
Notes   207

PREFACE
A Life-Altering Story

Have you ever read a book and become so absorbed in the story that it absorbs you? This has been my experience in writing *The Perfect Saviour*. This devotional helped save my life, because through the process of writing it, Jesus overwhelmed my heart with his love and enabled me to face the worst suffering I've ever experienced.

I began writing this devotional shortly before my wife, Linda, was diagnosed with Stage 4 ovarian cancer. In the beginning of our journey, we believed she'd be healed on this side of eternity, but God had a different plan. Eight months later, he took her home and healed her forever in heaven. Through it all, I've never doubted God's goodness. He's been with me every step of the way. In some ways, my journey has paralleled Jesus', only infinitesimally less intense.

As Jesus took his first step from Galilee towards Jerusalem, I began walking a road with him I'd never walked before—a road that would culminate in death. During the final week of his life, he entered the Holy City amidst celebration. Linda and I celebrated little victories early on as we believed God would heal her. When it became clear that, without a miracle, she wouldn't be healed, I joined Jesus in my own Gethsemane, agonizing in prayer, "Not my will, but yours be done."

He trudged up the hill to Golgotha, and I faced my spiritual and emotional form of crucifixion, dying to self, knowing my suffering could never compare to his. During those times when I felt like quitting, Linda spurred me on to continue writing, always believing in me.

Through it all, God hasn't failed me. I never cried, as Jesus did, "My God, my God, why have you forsaken me," because God hasn't forsaken me—and he never will. In that moment on the cross, Jesus faced hell for us. He felt the sting of God's rejection so none of us will ever have to experience the agony of being rejected by God.

Metaphorically, I feel as if I'm lying in a tomb awaiting the resurrection and asking myself, "How long must I endure this pain?" The days in this dark tomb of grief seem unending. But my hope doesn't waver. I know the resurrection is coming.

This is the message of *The Perfect Saviour*—hope. Hope in the midst of a dark world. Hope that, no matter what hell we face on earth, heaven awaits us. Hope that in the midst of a dark tomb, light will shine, life will return, and love will triumph.

If my story blesses you, then the agony I've endured is worth it. And if I, as a flawed human, feel this way, you can be sure this is immeasurably truer of Jesus. He was honoured to sacrifice his life for you. My prayer is that you'll encounter Jesus on every page of this book. May the *perfect Saviour* fill you with life and hope as you walk with him each step of your journey.

INTRODUCTION

On January 13, 1982, shortly after take off from Washington, DC, a Boeing 737 crashed into the Potomac River. Seventy-eight people perished in the icy waters. During rescue efforts, one of the surviving passengers, Arland D. Williams Jr., was handed a rope attached to a rescue helicopter. He selflessly passed it on to other passengers. He eventually died, sacrificing his life for strangers.[1]

We applaud heroes like Mr. Williams, who willingly died to save others. But as praiseworthy as his heroic efforts were, Jesus far surpassed his unselfish act. Jesus didn't die for strangers. He died for his enemies.

The apostle Paul wrote, "At just the right time, when we were still powerless, Christ died for the ungodly." Then he emphasised, "God demonstrates his own love for us in this: While we were still sinners, Christ died for us." Then, to be sure his readers didn't miss the point, he reiterated, "While we were God's enemies, we were reconciled to him through the death of his Son" (Romans 5:6, 8, 10).

Notice how Paul, under God's inspiration, describes us: "powerless . . . ungodly . . . sinners . . . enemies." Not very flattering. At this point, God could have acted as we probably would and written us off as a bunch of worthless sinners. But that's not how God responded. He saw our helpless situation, entered into our human condition, and sacrificed his life to save us—his enemies.

Unlike anyone else in history, Jesus was born to die. From the aeons of eternity, God planned it. Jesus' birth, childhood, and years as a carpenter prepared him for his mission. His three-year ministry propelled him towards the cross. Then he overcame death, rising three days after he was entombed. This singular accomplishment was the reason for everything he did.

As you read *The Perfect Saviour*, I pray you'll be captured by God's love for you. We'll begin with an eternal God and an eternal plan to unite us to himself. Then we'll follow Jesus as he "resolutely set out for Jerusalem" (Luke 9:51). We'll walk with Jesus through the last week of his life and stand alongside him through his arrest, betrayal, and trial. Then we'll stand at the cross as he dies for us. We'll conclude with Jesus walking out of the tomb and appearing in glory to his followers.

The final eight devotions in this book follow the days of Holy Week, so if you would like to follow this devotional through the season of Lent, then you should begin reading after Ash Wednesday. However, you may choose to read this book any time of year.

This devotional is divided into forty morning and evening meditations, with a bonus devotion at the end. Each reading contains a principle to consider, a question to ponder, a passage to explore, and a prayer to entreat. I invite you to soak in each daily devotion, open your heart, and let Jesus love you.

PART ONE

The Plan before Time

Long before he laid down earth's foundations, he had us in mind, had settled on us as the focus of his love, to be made whole and holy by his love. Long, long ago he decided to adopt us into his family through Jesus Christ. (What pleasure he took in planning this!) He wanted us to enter into the celebration of his lavish gift-giving by the hand of his beloved Son.

Ephesians 1:4–6 MSG

Just as [in His love] He chose us in Christ [actually selected us for Himself as His own] before the foundation of the world, so that we would be holy [that is, consecrated, set apart for Him, purpose-driven] and blameless in His sight.

Ephesians 1:4 AMP

A Preplanned Touchdown

Born with chromosomal Fragile X syndrome, Jake Porter is unable to read and can barely write. But he loves football and never missed a practice with Northwest High School in McDermott, Ohio. His coach, Dave Frantz, developed a plan to do something special for Jake in an upcoming game. He contacted Derek Dewitt, football coach at Waverly High. Assuming it wouldn't affect the score, Jake would carry the ball on the final play. He would take a knee and the game would end.

With five seconds left and Waverly leading 42–0, the coaches met at midfield with the refs, and modified their plan. Jake would be allowed to score. He came into the game, was given the ball, and began running. The Waverly defence parted like the Red Sea, allowing Jake to score a touchdown. Rick Reilly in *Sports Illustrated* wrote, "In the stands mothers cried and fathers roared. Players on both sidelines held their helmets to the sky and whooped."[1]

Imagine the joy in this young man's heart. A lot of planning occurred behind the scenes so he could experience the gift of a touchdown. The winning team paid the price by giving up six points and a shutout game. It wasn't much of a sacrifice considering they were ahead by forty-two points.

Think about God's plan. Before he created the universe, God purposed to save us. He knew we'd fail and determined to show us grace. But there was a price to pay, and it wasn't simply a touchdown. God himself would pay for our transgressions with his life.

Paul reminded us in Romans, "The wages of sin is death" (6:23). Because we've all sinned, we're all doomed (see 3:23). But God intervened with his marvellous plan. Because the price tag for sin is death, God would become a man, live a sinless life, and allow humanity to kill him. He planned the details before time began. Before he ever created us, before we ever sinned, God determined to rescue us from our self-imposed eternal disaster.

Just as the coaches developed a plan to show Jake Porter grace, extending undeserved favour towards us is the essence of God's eternal purpose, one he planned from all eternity and fulfilled in Christ Jesus. For the next few days, we'll consider various angles of God's eternal plan—a peek behind the curtains into what God was up to. Ages of planning so we could score a touchdown on Easter morning.

Principle

From all eternity, God planned to save us.

Ponder

- At what times do you most appreciate God's grace?
- When have you found yourself in a situation where someone extended grace to you, showing you favour you didn't deserve?

Pursue: For a deeper dive, study Romans 3:21–31.

Lord God, thank you for your grace. I praise you for your eternal plan of salvation. Now, because of your grace, I have the hope of eternal life.

Working behind the Scenes

At a small school in Washington, as the story is told, a group of twelve-year-old girls were beginning to wear lipstick. After applying it in the toilets, they pressed their mouths to the mirror, leaving dozens of lip prints. Each night the maintenance man removed them, and the next day, the girls repeated the process. They ignored the principal's appeals to "cease and desist." But there was more to the story, and they had no idea what was happening behind the scenes.

Finally, the principal summoned the young ladies into the toilets, with the maintenance man present. He explained again the trouble their cosmetology exercise was creating, then asked the custodian to show the girls the effort required to clean the mirror. Taking out a long-handled squeegee, he dipped it in the toilet, and cleaned the mirror. The result? No more lip prints.[2]

We're often shocked to discover what's occurring behind the scenes in a situation. These girls were clueless as to what the custodian was up to each evening.

In a strange way, this story parallels God's secret plan to save us. From all eternity, God was working behind the scenes, developing a plan for our salvation. Paul told the Ephesians, "He chose us in him before the creation of the world to be holy and blameless in his sight" (Ephesians 1:4).

What does this mean? It's a mystery too deep to fathom. Our human brains nearly explode, attempting to grasp a plan with no beginning. Father, Son, and Holy Spirit, forever joined in a divine dance stretching across the aeons. From the timeless depths of eternity, the Trinity, unlimited by time and space, always had a plan to make us one with them.

In the midst of the mystery, here's what we know. God didn't wait for Adam and Eve to sin before he acted. His indescribable plan was in effect before creating the universe. Then at the perfect time, God pulled back the curtain and gave us a glimpse of his intentions. Like these twelve-year-old girls, we gasp in amazement at what's been occurring behind the scenes—except, we gasp in a breathtaking way.

Let's embrace the marvel of the mystery. The elegance of the enigma. The weird and the wonderful. God's plan is a jaw-dropping thriller. Sure, those girls were in shock because of what they didn't see. But that doesn't begin to compare to how awestruck we are as we attempt to grasp God's plan before time.

Principle

From all eternity, God was working behind the scenes on a wonderful plan to save us.

Ponder

- When have you experienced a surprise or discovered something shocking that happened behind the scenes?
- What amazes you most about God's "Plan before Time"?

Pursue: For a deeper dive, study Ephesians 1:3–14.

Eternal God, your wisdom and purposes amaze me. My heart is filled with praise as I consider your plan before time.

It's All About You

The Broadway musical, *Man of La Mancha*, tells the story of Don Quixote, who sees himself as a knight riding through the countryside and battling windmills, which he imagines to be dragons. He performs these outlandish tasks to win the affection of a common prostitute named Aldonza, whom he renames Dulcinea, meaning "sweetness." The victim of repeated abuse, she's hard and cynical—anything but sweetness. But in Quixote's eyes, she is his beautiful princess. In the end, his unconditional love transforms the unworthy Aldonza into Dulcinea, his "Sweetness."

This is our story. I am Aldonza. You are Aldonza. We often prostitute ourselves before the idols of the world, yet in God's eyes, his people are like the pure and spotless Dulcinea (see Ephesians 5:25–27).

This truth is woven throughout Scripture. In Numbers 24, a king hired Balaam the prophet to curse God's people. Balaam stood on a hill overlooking Israel's camp and opened his mouth. But instead of allowing Balaam to curse them, he caused a blessing to pass through Balaam's lips. "How beautiful are your tents, Jacob, your dwelling places, Israel! Like valleys they spread out, like gardens beside a river" (vv. 5–6). This was how God regarded his people—the disobedient lot who prostituted themselves before other gods.

Throughout the millennia, as God's plan unfolded, he's always had his eye on his chosen people. He selected Abraham's family and sent his Son through the patriarch's descendants, the Israelites (Genesis 12:1–3). He gave them a context for the need for a blood sacrifice through the Passover. When his people repeatedly sinned, he disciplined them but always restored them. Finally the moment came, and Jesus entered our world (Galatians 4:4).

We've all heard the saying, "It's not about you." But in this case, it's *all* about you. Like Quixote, who did everything to win Dulcinea, God's eternal purpose has always been pointed towards saving each of us. When we understand this—deep inside—our lives are forever changed. Like Aldonza, no longer are we a hardened prostitute, abused by the world. We are Dulcinea, God's Sweetness.

All God's promises, all the prophecies, all his plans were for the singular purpose of saving us. I can't possibly grasp the depth of God's love. His breathtaking plan, stretching from eternity to eternity, really is all about me—and you!

Principle

God sees us as his beautiful Sweetness and carried out an eternal plan to save us.

Ponder

- How does knowing that God sees you as his Sweetness change your life?
- Likewise, how does knowing that God's plan is "all about you" impact you every day?

Pursue: For a deeper dive, study Numbers 22–24.

Lord God, thank you that you envisioned me before the world began as your beautiful Sweetness. I praise you for your marvellous plan that is "all about me." I'm awestruck at your love, which transforms me from Aldonza into Dulcinea. Help me see myself through your eyes.

Of Matchless Worth

In 2017, a painting by Renaissance master Leonardo da Vinci fetched a record price of $450.3 million at an auction. *Salvator Mundi* depicts Jesus holding an orb in his left hand with his right hand raised in blessing. Auctioned at Christie's in New York, the picture's price far surpassed that of any other work of art ever sold. Incredibly, in 1958, this canvas creation sold for only $59, because it was considered a fake.[3]

Call me uncultured, but I'm pretty sure I'm not the only one scratching his head over this story. How is it possible for any painting to be worth nearly half a billion bucks? Only one reason. The new owner saw such great value in the work of art he was willing to plop down $450,300,000 to prove it.

In some ways, we resemble that work of art. Half a billion dollars may seem like a lot to spend for a painted piece of canvas, but it's mere pocket change compared to the price God paid for each of us. The apostle Peter reminded believers, "For you know that God paid a ransom to save you from the empty life you inherited from your ancestors. And it was not paid with mere gold or silver, which lose their value. It was the precious blood of Christ, the sinless, spotless Lamb of God. God chose him as your ransom long before the world began" (1 Peter 1:18–20 NLT).

Before God ever created anything, before he said, "Let there be light," something existed. Pull back the curtains of eternity, and there it lay. The only thing in existence . . . a lamb. Sacrificed. But not just any lamb. The one and only sinless Lamb of God, Jesus Christ.

No price is higher, no entity more precious, nothing of greater worth than the life of God himself. This was the price God paid for each of us. Why? He considers our eternal destiny of greater value than the life of his own Son.

Why would we matter so much to him? I'm as bewildered as anyone else. But when the world screams, "You don't matter," reflect on this truth. When you feel devalued because you don't measure up to human standards, remember that God paid the ultimate price for you—with the precious blood of his only Son. This ought to leave us speechless. Each one of us is so valuable in God's eyes that he sacrificed his life in exchange for ours.

Principle

From all eternity, God had a plan to pay the ultimate price for us—the sacrifice of his Son.

Ponder

- What words would you use to describe how you feel about the price God was willing to pay for you?
- How can this knowledge help you when you feel devalued by the world?

Pursue: For a deeper dive, study 1 Peter 1:13–21.

> *Lord God, I'm speechless when I consider the price you were willing to pay for me. Remind me of this truth when I feel beaten down by the world around me.*

Angels Gone Wild

When I was eight, my cousin gave me a baseball card—some guy named Carl, who played for the Boston Red Sox. Turned out to be Carl Yastrzemski's rookie card, today valued at nearly $1,000. I made the error of gluing it into a scrapbook, which severely damaged the card. It's now worth about ten bucks. Without realising it, I failed to value something precious.

It's easy to undervalue God's plan as well. Christ followers experience the culmination of this plan. Peter described the mystery of this plan by stating that prophets "searched intently" to understand it. Then he added this cryptic statement: "Even angels long to look into these things" (1 Peter 1:10, 12). They long to understand the mystery of God's plan, which we receive freely.

Imagine angels observing the Eternal One creating the world. He held the universe in the palm of his hand (Isaiah 40:12) and directed his attention to an infinitesimal speck, within a speck, within a speck, called Earth. Perhaps the angels said to one another, "What on earth [literally] is God doing?" He went to work, creating—scooping out the oceans and uniquely shaping giraffes and elephants. I picture angels gasping in amazement. Then God took soil and shaped it into a mud man. He breathed on it, and it moved. The angels' jaws must have dropped as they stared in awe.

What do you suppose they thought when the newly created humans disobeyed God's only commandment? "Why didn't he destroy them?" some of them may have asked. As God's plan unfolded through the centuries, he nurtured and loved his people, showering them with grace when they least deserved it.

Can you imagine what might have gone through the angels' minds when God's Son left heaven and was born as a baby? And when he was crucified? In unison, they might have grabbed their swords, ready to destroy humankind, but God held them back. Perhaps the angels were mystified, trying to understand what God was up to. When Jesus rose from the dead, did their eyes finally open to glimpse God's plan?

So what do we possess today? Nothing much. Only something angels have gone wild over for thousands of years.

I blew it when I failed to value something great and glued Yaz's rookie card in a scrapbook. I don't want to make the same mistake with God's eternal plan, stick it away somewhere, and forget it. It's incomparably greater than a $1,000 baseball card. If you doubt this, just ask an angel. They've treasured God's plan for countless ages.

Principle

We possess something so valuable that angels have gone wild longing to understand it.

Ponder

- In what ways might you take God's eternal plan for granted?
- What steps can you take to treat this incredible gift with more respect?

Pursue: For a deeper dive, study 1 Peter 1:3–12.

> *Lord God, open my eyes to better understand your plan of salvation. Help me never take it for granted.*

Judge and Jury

In Wichita, Kansas, a man appeared in court for a speeding ticket. When he arrived, the court was closed due to heavy snowfall. Three days later, the clerk received this letter: "I was scheduled to be in court Feb. 23 concerning a traffic ticket. Well, I was there as scheduled. And to my surprise I was the only one there. No one called and told me the court would be closed. After going through the snow to be there on time, I decided to go ahead with the hearing as scheduled, which meant I had to be the accuser (the patrolman who gave me the citation) and I had to be the accused and also the judge.

"The citation was for going 46 mph in a 35–mph zone. . . . As the accuser, I felt that I was going over 35 mph, but as the accused I knew I was not going 46 mph, and as the judge, and being the understanding man that I am, I decided to throw it out of court this time, but it had better not happen again."[4]

One day, we'll all have an appointment in God's court. "Each of us will give an account of ourselves to God" (Romans 14:12). Don't you wish we could be our own judge? But this doesn't work, does it? God alone dispenses justice in the court of heaven.

Why doesn't God simply overlook our sin? Because a perfect God can't ignore wrongdoing—not even a little. Imagine an oncologist telling a patient, "You only have cancer in 10 percent of your body. No big deal." Or an employer testing a worker for drugs and ignoring a small amount of methamphetamines.

So God devised a perfect plan—the Judge would take upon himself the guilt of our crimes. He'd pay our ransom and die in our place, cancelling our debt of sin (Colossians 2:14). God doesn't ignore our sins. Instead, his plan called for the Judge to become the accused and receive the penalty for our crimes.

Jesus was made guilty so we could be declared innocent. He has removed our sins "as far as the east is from the west" (Psalm 103:12). We don't need to manipulate the court, like the man from Kansas. We simply need to trust that Jesus has removed our guilt, and paid the penalty for our sin. And we don't need a snowstorm to make this happen!

Principle

God devised a perfect plan to save us by paying the penalty for our crimes.

Ponder

- In what ways do you attempt to declare yourself "not guilty" rather than simply accept Christ's offer of salvation?
- On a scale of one to ten, how much do you trust in God's plan to save you, rather than your own cleverness—like the man from Kansas?

Pursue: For a deeper dive, study Romans 5:1–11.

Lord, thank you for determining to pay the debt for my crimes before I was even born. I know I'm guilty of numerous crimes against you, but I freely accept your "not guilty" verdict and your gift of eternal life.

Of Flying Refrigerators and Prophecy

W e've all made guesses about future events. But sometimes even the best of us miss the mark by a mile.

- In 1900, Smithsonian curator John Watkins predicted the future existence of "fast-flying refrigerators."
- In 1911, Thomas Edison declared that in the future "it will be an easy matter to convert a truckload of iron bars into virgin gold."
- In 1955, Alex Lewyt, president of Lewyt Vacuum Company, proclaimed that nuclear-powered vacuum cleaners would be a reality in ten years.[5]

In contrast, imagine more than three hundred prophecies about one man, fulfilled hundreds of years later. Impossible! Exactly. But this is precisely the case with Jesus.[6]

Consider the prophecies relating just to his death. Jesus would be betrayed for thirty pieces of silver, which was returned and used to buy a potter's field (Zechariah 11:12–13). He'd remain silent when accused, be denied justice, receive a beating, be smitten and spat upon, die for our sins, and be buried with the rich (Isaiah 53:4–9). He would be stripped of his clothing, men would gamble for his robe, and his hands and feet would be pierced (Psalm 22:16–18).

Should I continue? We can't dismiss this tiny sample of those more than three hundred prophecies. The odds of fulfilling just eight of them is one in ten to the seventeenth power. For perspective, imagine covering the state of Texas in silver dollars two-feet thick, with one of them marked. Then walk through Texas and pick one up. The odds of getting the marked silver dollar is equivalent to the possibility of Jesus fulfilling only eight of these prophecies.[7]

God's plan is even more marvellous than we imagined. When he planned our salvation, he didn't wait for events to unfold. He inspired prophets to paint a detailed picture of the coming Messiah—three hundred–plus prophecies spelling out the tiniest detail about his life. Right down to how he would die, hundreds of years before crucifixion was even invented!

It's comforting to know, in our unstable world, that we can have confidence in Jesus and trust every word of the Bible. No human could possibly have made that many educated guesses. We can securely rest, knowing God sees our future. It's in his hands. And God can say, "I told you so."

Principle

Bible prophecy demonstrates how incredible God's plan is.

Ponder

- When have you predicted something—and guessed accurately? When have you been wrong?
- In what ways does fulfilled biblical prophecy give you security in Jesus and the Bible?

Pursue: For a deeper dive, study Psalm 22.

All-Seeing God, you alone know the future. Thank you for giving me the evidence of fulfilled prophecy to strengthen my faith. Help me trust you more, knowing my future is in your hands.

Cheering for All Eternity

Our granddaughter, Tesia, was performing in a piano recital along with other first graders. One by one, young entertainers approached the stage and tickled the ivories, attempting to make musical magic at the keyboard. Sitting through this melodic extravaganza wasn't easy. If the students had scraped their nails on chalkboards, they might have produced more pleasant sounds.

Yet as each pianist completed their performance, guess how the audience responded? With applause. At the end, the children garnered a standing ovation. Why in the name of Paderewski would we reward such a performance? Because the room loved these young musicians. We weren't applauding the quality of their performance. We were cheering for their effort—despite the fact that it offended our ears.

Think about God's plan to save us. Before we did anything—good or bad—he was cheering for us. Not because of our outstanding performance, but because of the love he already felt for us before we were born. Before we ever pounded a sour note, he was cheering in advance. It's beautiful music to him. Even when we don't get it right. Even when we mess up royally. Even when our best efforts mirror a first-grade piano recital. Psalm 147:11 states, "The LORD delights in those who fear him, who put their hope in his unfailing love."

Our love for our kids and grandkids despite their imperfect musical efforts is a lot like God's love for us. The psalmist said, "The Lord takes pleasure in those who fear him, in those who hope in his steadfast love" (Psalm 147:11 ESV). He doesn't cheer us on in the Christian life because of our outstanding performance, because we don't always get it right. Some days we mess up, and our best efforts resemble a first-grade piano recital.

Thankfully, God's love isn't based on what we do, but on what he did for us. "He saved us, not because of righteous things we had done, but because of his mercy" (Titus 3:5). Likewise, I celebrated Tesia because she's my granddaughter, and I love her.

Does God overlook sin? Absolutely not. This is why Jesus came. But even knowing from all eternity how poorly we'd perform, he persevered to save us. Today, he's on the front row loving us and cheering us on, like a proud papa. Even when our sour notes wreak havoc on everyone's ears.

As we close this section, pause and reflect on God's incredible plan. From all eternity, he planned to save us by paying the ultimate price for us with his Son's life. He intervened throughout history to bring it to pass. His greatest desire was to restore us. Not because we'd perform well, but because of his love for us.

Got it? Me neither . . . God's plan is a mystery too profound to grasp.

Principle

God's plan to save us wasn't based on how well we would perform but on his love for us.

Ponder

- Under what circumstances are you most likely to beat yourself up because of your poor performance?
- How does understanding God's unconditional love for you despite your performance help you overcome your struggles?

Pursue: For a deeper dive, study Romans 8:31–39.

Heavenly Father, thank you for not rejecting me because of my poor performance. I thank you for your marvellous plan and the knowledge that you take delight in me, even when I hit sour notes.

PART TWO

The Journey
with Jesus

*Jesus took the Twelve aside and told them, "We
are going up to Jerusalem, and everything that is
written by the prophets about the Son of Man will
be fulfilled. He will be delivered over to the Gentiles.
They will mock him, insult him and spit on him;
they will flog him and kill him. On the third day he
will rise again." The disciples did not understand
any of this. Its meaning was hidden from them, and
they did not know what he was talking about.*

Luke 18:31–34

*For surely if Christ was not God, he was not a good
man either, since he plainly said he was God.*

Sir Thomas More[1]

"Who Do You Say I Am?" (Part 1)

Years ago, our youth pastor conducted a survey on a local college campus, asking students, "Who was Jesus?" A few answered, "The Son of God." One or two didn't believe Jesus ever existed. But the overwhelming response was, "A great man." This reflects the view of most folks in our culture.

As Jesus prepared for his final journey to Jerusalem, he took his disciples aside and asked them, "Who do you say I am?" (Matthew 16:15). Peter responded spot-on. "You are the Messiah, the Son of the living God" (v. 16).

Of all the questions we could ask, "Who is Jesus?" is probably foremost. Yet many folks skate through life, never giving the question serious thought. So, who was Jesus—merely a great man or much, much more?

Consider this. Great men don't claim to be God as Jesus did. If you met me, and my first words were, "Hi, I'm God, and I created the universe," you might be more than a little scared. You might even say to yourself, "I hope he doesn't have any weapons with him, because he's nuts."

Yet this is *exactly* what Jesus claimed. As he talked with Nicodemus, Jesus declared himself to be God's "one and only Son" (John 3:16). Notice he didn't claim to be *a* son of God—but the *only* Son of God. He's saying, "Of all the billions of people who will ever walk this planet, I am the only one who is not *only* a human being. I am God in human form."

But Jesus didn't stop there. In John 5, he claimed to be the life giver

(v. 21). He says he'll judge mankind (v. 22), we must believe in him for eternal life (v. 24), and he'll raise the dead (vv. 28–29). These are qualities and abilities only God possesses.

C. S. Lewis wrote, "A man who was merely a man and said the sort of things Jesus said would not be a great moral teacher. He would either be a lunatic, on a level with the man who says he is a poached egg, or else he would be the Devil of Hell. . . . Let us not come up with any patronizing nonsense about His being a great human teacher. He has not left that open to us. He did not intend to."[2]

We'll examine this further in the next devotion.

Principle

Jesus could not have been merely a great man because great men don't claim to be God.

Ponder

- Who do you believe Jesus is?
- Have you ever considered that Jesus can't be merely a great man because of the claims he made? How does this influence what you believe about him?

Pursue: For a deeper dive, study John 5:16–30.

Lord Jesus, I confess my faith in you. You are the one and only Son of God. I invite you to be my Saviour, and I surrender my life to you.

"Who Do You Say I Am?" (Part 2)

Imagine a police captain sending officers to arrest a man. Then picture them returning empty-handed. Imagine the captain asking them why they didn't arrest the man, and envision the officers replying, "Because no one ever spoke the way this man does."

Okay, no more imagining, because it's too bizarre to imagine.

But it's not. It happened with Jesus (John 7:46).

In the previous evening's devotion, we focused on Jesus' claims to be God. Let's continue this exploration. Either his claims were true or false. If false, then there are two possibilities. One possibility—Jesus *knew* his claims were false, making him a liar. And even worse, he deliberately deceived multitudes into following him, all the while leading them to hell, making him incredibly evil.

Is this possible? Here's an evil man, a con man beyond any we could imagine, claiming to be God. He was arrested for claiming to be God. Put on trial for claiming to be God. And eventually put to death for, yes, claiming to be God. At some point, what's this self-absorbed egomaniac going to do? Tell the authorities "I'm not God." But Jesus didn't do that. Even though he had nothing to gain by dying, this narcissistic cult leader allowed himself to be killed. Which makes no sense.

Here's another possibility—Jesus did *not* know his claims were false. He *believed* he was God, which would make him a lunatic. Is this possible? Jesus, the Master Teacher, who gave the world its greatest moral standard, who made fools of the greatest intellectuals of his time, was a raving lunatic? Doesn't add up.

But there's a third possibility—Jesus was who he claimed to be. Not a liar, not a lunatic, but Lord of all.[3] By process of elimination, this is the only logical conclusion. But beyond this, examine the life of Jesus: his teachings, his actions, and his miracles. When you read the testimonies of witnesses and see the millions of lives that have been transformed through the centuries by the teachings of Jesus, you realise he was more than a carpenter. He was, as he claimed to be, God in human form.

We can rely on Jesus. We can trust him, knowing every word he says is true. I challenge you to read the fifth, sixth, and seventh chapters of Matthew, even if you've read them before. You'll arrive at the same conclusion as the temple police two thousand years ago, "No one ever spoke the way this man does" (John 7:46).

Principle

Jesus was neither a liar nor a lunatic. He is who he claimed to be—God.

Ponder

- What specific teaching of Jesus causes you to say, "No one ever spoke the way this man does"?
- If you had been one of the Jewish authorities, how would you have reacted to the temple police's comment about why they didn't arrest Jesus?

Pursue: For a deeper dive, study John 7:25–52.

> *Lord Jesus, I worship you as the Son of God. I embrace*
> *your teachings with all my heart because I know that*
> *no mere human could have spoken those words.*

Jesus Resolutely Set Out

You've been planning a hike for months—five nights of spectacular scenery, sleeping under the stars, breathing in the fresh air of God's creation. (If you're not a hiker, pretend you are for a few minutes.) Your nostrils dance with delight, imagining the fresh scent of pine needles and campfire smoke curling upward towards heaven. But suppose, as you're leaving, God supernaturally reveals that your trip will end in disaster and death. There's no doubt it's true. Knowing that, would you still go?

Jesus did. "As the time approached for him to be taken up to heaven, Jesus resolutely set out for Jerusalem" (Luke 9:51). Fully aware that his journey would deposit him in the throes of arrest, torture, and death, Jesus was unwavering in his determination.

If I were Jesus (thankfully, for humanity's sake, I'm not), I couldn't have forced my legs to take even one step towards such a doomed fate. How did he feel as he trudged along the road through Galilee, Perea, down to Jericho, and eventually up the winding hill into Jerusalem—knowing each sandal mark he left on the dusty road brought him a tiny bit closer to a torturous death?

But he pressed on towards the cross. Why? Because his death would pay for our depravity. There was no other way. Did he see our faces as he trudged that highway—alone, even though mobbed by crowds, because no one understood? At least three times, he told his disciples that "he must be killed and after three days rise again" (Mark 8:31, for example). But they were clueless.

Jesus chose his destiny for one simple reason. His purpose was worth the price. He laid down his life "for the joy set before him" (Hebrews

12:2). The joy of what he accomplished in dying for us was greater than the pain. To him, we were worth it.

As we join Jesus on his final journey, we'll be immersed in adventure—both heartwarming and heartbreaking. We'll meet a man who couldn't see (and couldn't stop talking), a businessman who scampered up a tree in a first-century Gucci suit, a dead man who couldn't stay buried, a donkey who carved his niche in history, and a Saviour whose love has never been equalled. Nothing could stop Jesus when he "resolutely set out for Jerusalem."

Principle

Jesus determined to go to Jerusalem because we were worth the price of his sacrifice.

Ponder

- If you had been Jesus on the highway to Jerusalem, how would you have felt?
- How does knowing that the joy of redeeming us was greater than Jesus' pain inspire you to live for him?

Pursue: For a deeper dive, study Mark 8:32–34.

Lord Jesus, thank you for being willing to take that final journey to Jerusalem, knowing it would end in your death. I worship and praise you for choosing to save me.

Holding Your Breath

On March 27, 2021, Budimir Sobat of Croatia achieved something no other human has ever accomplished. He held his breath for twenty-four minutes, thirty-seven seconds, setting a new world record. How is this humanly possible?[4]

Martha and Mary must have been holding their breath as they waited for Jesus. The last stop on his final journey to Jerusalem was probably their home in Bethany. The two sisters urged Jesus to hurry because their brother was gravely ill. They sent word: "Lord, the one you love is sick" (John 11:3). And Jesus received the message: "So when he heard that Lazarus was sick . . ."

How would we expect the next phrase to read? Perhaps "he hurried there immediately." Instead, ". . . he stayed where he was two more days" (v. 6).

So Jesus deliberately stayed behind? Why? Because unbeknownst to everyone else, he intended to raise Lazarus from the dead. Upon arriving, Martha told Jesus, "If you had been here, my brother would not have died" (v. 21). There's a lot of pain behind these words. She's asking, "Lord, why did you wait so long?"

Ever feel like Martha—like you needed God to show up yesterday? Instead, he's four days late, and you're gasping for air. Perhaps you're waiting for a job promotion, a difficult marriage to heal, a health issue to resolve, or a teenager to grow up. You want something to happen. Anything. You're gasping for air. You've reached the twenty-four-minute mark, and you're barely hanging on.

But God's timing is always perfect. He's always on time, even when we think he's too late. When we feel like we've been holding our breath forever, he has something planned he never would have accomplished if he'd acted when we wanted him to.

Most of us find waiting on the Lord one of the most difficult tasks God asks of us. But the other options—wringing our hands in fear or being angry with him for not showing up when we think he should—are a surefire way to say goodbye to peace in our life. Waiting doesn't mean we sit and do nothing. The Hebrew word for *wait* comes from a root word meaning "entwine." We entwine ourselves with God. We surrender our burdens to him and trust his timing, because God's timing is always perfect. Even when he's four days late. Even when we're reaching the twenty-four-minute mark and gasping for air.

Principle

Waiting on the Lord is hard, but trusting his perfect timing is the only way we can have peace in a difficult situation.

Ponder

- In what circumstances do you find it the most difficult to wait on the Lord?
- During these times, what helps you experience his peace?

Pursue: For a deeper dive, study John 11:1–22.

Lord Jesus, give me the strength to wait on you in difficult times. Help me entwine myself in you, trust your perfect timing, and surrender to your will.

Empty

After decades of counselling teens, psychologist Madeline Levine is seeing a barrage of despondent youth—mostly successful and advantaged kids—feeling lost and empty. In *The Price of Privilege*, she tells of a fifteen-year-old girl who was "bright, personable, highly pressured by her adoring, but frequently preoccupied . . . parents," yet was "very angry." Levine diagnosed her as a "cutter." On one of her arms, the teen had carved the word *EMPTY* with a razor.[5]

Mark writes of a similar person, a rich young ruler, who ran up to Jesus and asked how he could obtain eternal life. After Jesus answered him, Scripture tells us, "Jesus looked at him and loved him." Then Jesus told the young ruler to give everything he owned to the poor and follow him. "At this the man's face fell. He went away sad, because he had great wealth" (Mark 10:21–22).

In some ways, this rich ruler's life parallels that of Levine's young client and millions of others. They seek what the world offers, which leaves them empty. How many are moving through life as mere shells with *EMPTY* carved, not into their skin, but on their hearts? How many are unaware of the abundant life God offers (John 10:10)? How many sense something's missing but can't identify it? Joy and peace lie just beyond their grasp, like a carrot dangling on a stick.

What's the answer? It's Jesus, pure and simple. He is the Light of the World (John 8:12), the Bread of Life (John 6:35), and the giver of Living Water (John 4:10). He fills every longing of our empty hearts.

On one occasion, when the multitudes had abandoned Jesus, he asked his disciples, "You do not want to leave too, do you?" (John 6:67). Simon Peter replied, "Lord, to whom shall we go? You have the words of eternal life" (v. 68). Let me paraphrase: "If not Jesus, then what?" The wealth of the rich young ruler or any other idol Satan dangles before us will leave us empty and dry. The world simply cannot fulfil us.

Scripture doesn't mention the rich young ruler again. But we can be sure of this: his wealth never satisfied the emptiness in his heart. It can't. Seeking fulfilment in anything other than Jesus leaves us frustrated, fearful, and . . . empty.

Principle
Pursuing what the world offers leaves us empty.

Ponder
- What worldly fulfilment sometimes entices you?
- Under what circumstances do you truly grasp the reality of "If not Jesus, then what?"

Pursue: For a deeper dive, study Mark 10:17–31.

> *Lord Jesus, I confess that at times my heart is drawn to what the world offers. During those moments, please prompt me through your Spirit to seek you instead.*

"Cinderella, It's Me!"

Imagine your deepest desire being fulfilled in an instant. For a five-year-old girl, fantasy became reality at Disneyland. The girl (we'll call her Suzie) was enamoured with Cinderella. Her dream was to interact with the famed Disney princess at the Magic Kingdom. But after a long day of connecting with other characters, they hadn't experienced any Cinderella sightings. That evening, during the Main Street parade, the family watched as float after float went by, hoping to catch a glimpse of Suzie's heroine. Near the end, Suzie spotted Cinderella's float. She began shouting and waving, "Cinderella . . . Cinderella!" Engulfed in a noisy crowd, Cinderella could not hear Suzie.

She called even louder, "Cinderella, it's me, Suzie." She continued shouting and waving, to no avail. Then something magical occurred. The crowd around Suzie joined her cause, shouting to draw Cinderella's attention to Suzie. Eventually, Cinderella turned her head, stretched out her hand towards Suzie, and, looking her adoring fan in the eyes, said, "Hi, Suzie!" The crowd erupted with a cheer. You can only imagine the thrill that filled young Suzie's heart.

Heading to Jerusalem to commence the final week of his life, Jesus was experiencing a Cinderella-like ordeal. Like a celebrity in a parade, he was followed by a crowd. As he passed through Jericho, a blind beggar named Bartimaeus called out to him, "Jesus, Son of David, have mercy on me!" (Mark 10:47). The crowd following Jesus rebuked the blind man "and told him to be quiet" (v. 48). But like Suzie, the beggar shouted even louder. And like Cinderella, Jesus turned and faced him. Then Jesus healed Bartimaeus. His persistence paid off.

Scripture tells us to persevere in prayer. I wonder how often Jesus waits for us to persistently call out to him. If Suzie and Bartimaeus had failed to persevere, imagine the blessing they would have missed. Matthew 7:7 states, "Keep on asking, and you will receive what you ask for. Keep on seeking, and you will find. Keep on knocking, and the door will be opened to you" (NLT). "Pray continually" (1 Thessalonians 5:17).

Who is your Cinderella? What is the deepest desire of your heart? For Jesus to heal your body? Your broken heart? Your marriage? Our nation? Cry out to Jesus. Like Bartimaeus. Like Suzie. And don't quit. Look to heaven and cry out, "Jesus, it's me!"

Principle

God hears us as we persevere in prayer.

Ponder

- What is your Cinderella, the deepest desire of your heart?
- On a scale of one to ten, how persistently do you call out to Jesus?

Pursue: For a deeper dive, study Mark 10:46–52.

Lord Jesus, you know the deepest desire of my heart. I lift this to you right now. Hear my cry, Lord, and answer my prayer.

Ministering to the Lost

Zacchaeus ran as fast as his legs could carry him—his exquisitely crafted robe flapping in the breeze. Crowds thronged Main Street, hoping to catch a glimpse of Jesus. Zacchaeus jumped. And jumped again, but he was short. He couldn't peer above the masses. Then he spotted a tree. He sprinted and leapt, barely catching a low-hanging limb. He pushed his body up and over. Just in time. The popular rabbi was heading in his direction.

Then the rabbi stopped—right in front of the short man's tree. Jesus looked up, probably chuckled, and said, "Zacchaeus, come down immediately. I must stay at your house today" (Luke 19:5). The crowd must have gasped at the rabbi's offer to enter such a notorious sinner's home. Zacchaeus "came down at once and welcomed him gladly" (v. 6).

Can you feel the day's excitement? The message is clear. Of all the people in Jericho, Zacchaeus might have least deserved a visit from Jesus. First-century tax collectors were a notorious lot. Not only traitors who sold out their fellow countrymen by working for the Roman government but also thieves who padded their pockets by overcharging their neighbours—folks already overburdened with Rome's taxes. And he wasn't *just* a tax collector. To make matters worse, he was a *chief* tax collector. The vilest of the vile.

But Jesus saw something in Zacchaeus that no one else could. A heart ready to repent. So Zacchaeus came down from his perch. As the crowd listened on, Zacchaeus made a profound announcement. "Here and now I give half of my possessions to the poor, and if I have cheated anybody out of anything, I will pay back four times the amount" (v. 8). I bet that left folks scrambling for their tax statements.

Jesus responded, "Today salvation has come to this house, because this man, too, is a son of Abraham. For the Son of Man came to seek and to save the lost" (vv. 9–10).

Of all statements in Scripture, perhaps this most succinctly captures the mission of Jesus—"to seek and to save the lost." Isn't this our mission as well? (Matthew 28:19). So, what are we waiting for? Rather than judging others as unworthy, let's look at people through God's eyes. Let's go out, find a Zacchaeus, and minister to the lost.

Principle

Rather than judging others as unworthy, let's look at people through God's eyes.

Ponder

- In what ways is Jesus calling you to minister to the lost?
- Who in your life is like Zacchaeus, someone you might reach out to?

Pursue: For a deeper dive, study Luke 19:1–10.

Lord, open my eyes to the needs around me, especially to those like Zacchaeus, whom I might consider the least deserving of your grace.

Not Allowed to Die

In 2008, the mayor of a village in southwest France threatened residents with severe punishment if they died, because there was no room left in the crowded cemetery to bury them. Based on a county ordinance, Mayor Gerard Lalanne told the 260 residents of Sarpourenx, "All persons not having a plot in the church cemetery and wishing to be buried there are forbidden from dying in the parish. . . . Offenders will be severely punished."[6]

Not allowed to die? I'd like to know how Mayor Lalanne intended to enforce that law and what the punishment would be for a dead person who broke it! Pass all the laws you want against dying, but deciding not to die is not an option.

However, setting aside our human paradigm of life and death, Jesus went even further than this mayor. Jesus promised his followers they would never die. After Lazarus's death, Jesus told his sister Martha, "I am the resurrection and the life. The one who believes in me will live, even though they die; and whoever lives by believing in me will never die" (John 11:25–26).

It's not an overstatement to claim that this is the most astounding statement ever uttered. Think about those words: "You . . . will . . . never . . . die." What could be more powerful? What could be more profound? Eternal life is the dream of humankind. Ponce de Leon died trudging through the swamps of Florida, seeking the fabled Fountain of Youth. But who needs the Fountain of Youth? Because of Jesus, we can cast aside our fear of death and embrace eternal life.

How could Jesus make such an outlandish claim? When he rose from the grave, he conquered death. He stared it in the face and walked out of the tomb, never to die again. Because of his victory, he promises us eternal life. If we believe in him, we will never die.

Of course, we'll exit this world someday, but the experience will be like walking from one room into another. The *real* me and the *real* you will live forever. We'll experience a life far more wonderful than we've ever imagined.

Unlike the French mayor's injunction, we won't be punished for dying. Instead, by living in connection with Jesus, we'll be rewarded. We have God's word on it. Death is not an option. According to Jesus, we're not allowed to die.

Principle

Because of Jesus' resurrection, he promises that we'll live forever.

Ponder

- On a scale of one to ten, how much do you believe this promise of Jesus?
- How does this promise give you hope and comfort as you face difficulties and death?

Pursue: For a deeper dive, study John 11:23–31.

> *Lord Jesus, thank you for the promise that I'll live forever. During difficult times, fill my heart with this assurance.*

A Crying God

In Bible school, our instructor assigned us to memorize fifty verses from the gospel of John. I placed John 11:35, "Jesus wept," at the top of my list for one simple reason. It's the shortest verse in the Bible. But through the years, I've also come to appreciate it as one of the most meaningful.

A God who cries? That's bizarre. Who could imagine it? Exactly. This is why we know it's true. Humans wouldn't invent a crying God.

But when we ponder these two simple words, God comes alive for us in new ways. When Jesus came, he could have insulated himself from sadness, sorrow, and pain. But he intentionally chose to subject himself to every form of misery we endure. He wanted to feel what we feel, to hurt when we hurt, to struggle with our struggles. "Jesus wept."

When Jesus stood at the grave of his friend Lazarus, he wasn't crying because he missed him. Jesus knew his healing power would raise Lazarus to life. He cried because others who loved Lazarus cried. John records, "When Jesus saw [Mary] weeping, and the Jews who had come along with her also weeping, he was deeply moved in spirit and troubled" (11:33).

Sometimes we place expectations on God which he never promised—such as keeping bad things from happening to us. We become resentful because he doesn't come through in ways we think he should. But God hasn't promised to protect us from pain. Quite the opposite. In John 16:33, Jesus declares, "In this world you will have trouble."

God assures us of something greater than eliminating pain. He promises to be with us amid our troubles. "When you pass through the waters, I will be with you; and when you pass through the rivers, they will not sweep over you. When you walk through the fire, you will not be burned" (Isaiah 43:2). Notice he doesn't say *if* but *when*. In verse five, he adds, "Do not be afraid, for I am with you." Rather than standing back and watching us suffer, he hurls himself headfirst into our heartache.

When Jesus stood weeping with Lazarus's sisters, he was living out this promise in the flesh. He joined his friends in their sadness and sorrow. "Jesus wept." Two short words, packed with power, peace, and promise, because they reveal to us a God who cries with us in the pit of our pain.

Principle

God enters into our pain and grieves with us.

Ponder

- When has God entered into your sorrow and cried with you?
- How can you appreciate this comforting attribute of God in a deeper way?

Pursue: For a deeper dive, study John 11:32–44.

> *Lord Jesus, thank you that you don't stand back and watch me suffer. Thank you for being a God who cries with me. When I grieve, help me remember this.*

The Little Donkey

Donkeys. God really cares about these beasts of burden. Other than the serpent, donkeys are the only talking animal in Scripture (Numbers 22:28–35). They're mentioned 142 times in the Bible. Compare this with the word *grace*, which finds its place in holy writ a mere 124 times. (Okay, this proves nothing—it's just a fun fact.)

But eclipsing these honours, this four-legged beast is the animal Jesus selected for his triumphal entry. A specific donkey chosen by God, prophesied in Scripture 550 years before the event occurred. Zechariah 9:9 states, "Your king comes to you, righteous and victorious, lowly and riding on a donkey, on a colt, the foal of a donkey."

Picture the day. The streets were thronged with people, elbow to elbow. The noise must have rivalled that of the Super Bowl. Masses milled about, heading to the temple. Worshippers scurried as they selected their lambs for the Passover feast. How ironic that the Lamb of God rode into town that very day—seated on a donkey.

Let's pretend Little Donkey returned to his stable and shared with his mother all that had happened. "Mama, you won't believe what I did today! I carried a man into town. All these people came out to see me and stood on the side of the road waving palm branches. They cheered for me and even laid down their coats for me to walk on. They kept cheering until I arrived at the temple. You must be so proud of me!"

The wise mother replies, "Those people weren't cheering for you. They were praising the man you carried. He's the Messiah we've been waiting for. It was a great honour that God chose you to carry the King, but the praise doesn't belong to you. The glory is his alone!"

Ever find yourself playing the part of Little Donkey? Perhaps we seek the praise of people. But our only real honour lies in carrying Jesus to others. Second Corinthians 4:7 states, "We have this treasure in jars of clay to show that this all-surpassing power is from God and not from us."

Did you catch that? Like Little Donkey, God chose us to bring Jesus to the people. He entrusts his treasure to us. The real honour is that we carry Jesus to the masses around us. As our friend Little Donkey did, let's not lose sight of this.

Principle

Our only real honour lies in carrying Jesus to the masses.

Ponder

- In what situations have you found yourself full of donkey-like pride?
- What creative ways can you use to carry Jesus to your friends?

Pursue: For a deeper dive, study Matthew 21:1–11.

*Lord Jesus, thank you for the honour you've given me
to carry you to the masses. Help me remember that
glory and praise belong to you and you alone.*

PART THREE

The Night from Hell

After arriving in Jerusalem, Jesus spent the final week of his life teaching in the temple, serving the people, and resting to prepare for the huge challenges that lay before him.

Rather than considering his final week now, we'll explore it in Days 33–40. In this section, we'll focus on the final night of Jesus' life, when Satan and his minions unleashed their attacks against the Son of God. It was literally a night from hell.

Jesus, knowing all that was going to happen to him, went out.

John 18:4

So . . .

Ever notice the difference one little word can make? When I asked my wife to marry me, she said, "Yes," and my life was forever changed. In contrast, if someone pays you a compliment and adds the word *but*, what's almost certain to follow? A statement negating their adulation. Same with the Bible. Don't overlook the small words.

Consider the final night of Christ's life. As Jesus celebrated Passover with his disciples, he "knew that the Father had put all things under his power, and that he had come from God and was returning to God; *so* he got up from the meal, took off his outer clothing, and wrapped a towel around his waist. After that, he poured water into a basin and began to wash his disciples' feet" (John 13:3–5, emphasis added).

This little word *so* speaks volumes. Jesus understood his identity—who he was, where he came from, and where he was going—*so* he was able to humble himself and wash his disciples' feet. Jesus didn't need to prove anything to anyone. But the disciples? "A dispute also arose among them as to which of them was considered to be greatest" (Luke 22:24). That's why none of them were willing to wash one another's feet. They were so stuck in trying to prove their value and locked into their selfish mindsets, they never even considered the agony Jesus was facing.

If I were Jesus, I probably would have thrown a sandal at them, abandoned humanity, and returned to heaven. But because Jesus understood his identity, he not only endured the disciples' self-interest but also every form of abuse and torture that night contained.

Likewise, knowing who we are in relation to Christ empowers us to withstand insults and demeaning tasks. They hurt, but they don't devastate us. We allow God to define our identity, which enables us to serve others without fearing it makes us look bad. We don't need others' approval because God already approves of us—and his opinion is the only one that matters.

Self-pity, victimization, and low self-esteem disappear when we're anchored in our God-given identity. This is why we must remember who we are and who God made us to be. We are beloved children of the Creator. We are one with our Saviour. We are righteous and redeemed forever. *So* . . . how do we choose to respond?

Principle

Understanding our identity in Christ enables us to withstand the insults of others and serve those around us.

Ponder

- In what situations do you find your identity in Christ most threatened (feeling inadequate, insulted, making mistakes, etc.)?
- What aspects of your God-given identity can you recall to help you withstand these attacks?

Pursue: For a deeper dive, study John 13:1–16.

Lord, thank you for not only saving me but also redefining me. Help me find my identity in who you say I am rather than allowing others to determine my value.

The Father's House

When I was a boy, my family travelled to Nana's house in West Texas for Christmas. When we arrived, I stepped into a magical world. Besides Santa's visit, the pinnacle of the season was being together with relatives. They arrived on Christmas Eve—aunts, uncles, and cousins. Every room was abuzz with commotion. We played games, told stories, exchanged gifts, and ate tons of unhealthy foods. Available beds were scarce. I recall my dad placing two chairs seat-to-seat, wrapping me in a blanket, and laying me on them. I slept as if lying on a feather bed.

So much imagery of heaven is pictured as relationships—especially family. After the Last Supper, Jesus told his disciples he was leaving them. They were devastated. He reassured them, "Do not let your heart be troubled (afraid, cowardly). Believe [confidently] in God *and* trust in Him, [have faith, hold on to it, rely on it, keep going and] believe also in Me. In My Father's house are many dwelling places. If it were not so, I would have told you, because I am going there to prepare a place for you. And if I go and prepare a place for you, I will come back again and I will take you to Myself, so that where I am you may be also" (John 14:1–3 AMP).

This passage doesn't depict each of us living in our own mansion on a hilltop, where we'll pop in and visit each other occasionally. Most likely, Jesus is referencing a Jewish family compound, an *insula*, consisting of a courtyard surrounded by rooms. As each son married, he and his wife added a room adjacent to the courtyard. A perfect picture of community life, adding a richness to *house* we don't catch in our culture.[1]

The disciples would have recognised this metaphor as Jewish marriage language. When a couple was betrothed, the young man told his bride-to-be, "I go to prepare a place for you." He then began building their room in his father's insula.

In the challenging decades that lay ahead, the disciples would recall this conversation. How precious Christ's words must have been, with this rich description of heaven. How much hope this picture would bring these men, knowing their Master would return, bring them to the Father's house, and live with them forever. How encouraging this promise of Jesus is for us, assuring us that he will bring us home, where we will join him forever in the Father's house, alongside these heroes of faith.

Principle

One of the most beautiful descriptions of heaven is of our relationships with one another in the Father's house.

Ponder

- When have you experienced the joy of close relationships with family or friends?
- How does the picture of an insula increase your anticipation of life in heaven?

Pursue: For a deeper dive, study John 14:1–4.

> *Loving Father, thank you for the picture of living*
> *eternally in your insula with you and my family in*
> *Christ. With joy I anticipate that family reunion.*

"Show Us the Way"

In the days before cars and phones had a global positioning system (GPS), a young man from our church gave me directions to pick him up for a Bible study. I unfolded the paper on which he had drawn his map, and it left me in total confusion. It contained no words, simply a series of crisscross lines representing streets. I didn't even know which way was right side up. Frustrated, I picked up my phone, called him, and he met me on the highway. The return trip presented no challenges because he was seated next to me, telling me where to turn. I had no further need for his directions because the person himself became my road map.

Similarly, during the Last Supper, Jesus provided his disciples with a road map to God. He told them he was leaving and that they knew where he was going. Confused, they asked Jesus to show them the way. Jesus replied, "I am the way and the truth and the life. No one comes to the Father except through me" (John 14:6). He is the road map to the Father.

This statement trips up many folks because it sounds so narrow—and it is. But let's examine what Jesus is saying. Notice Jesus doesn't say *Christianity* is the only way to God, because it's not. Christianity is a system of beliefs practiced by followers of Jesus. No religious system will lead us to God, including Christianity.

But this doesn't solve the problem of Jesus appearing narrow-minded because any human setting himself forth as the *only* way to God seems astonishingly arrogant. And this would be true—if Jesus is just a man. But what if Jesus isn't comparing himself to other religious leaders such as Buddha and Muhammad? What if Jesus is God in human form, as he claims? "Anyone who has seen me has seen the Father" (v. 9).

If this is true, his claims would not only make sense, but would be exactly what we'd expect him to say. "You want to get to God? Well, here I am. Just connect your life to mine, and you'll be connected to God."

God not only sent Jesus to save us, he also sent him to guide us. This is significant in our confused and troubled world. We don't need more ideas, theories, or philosophies. We need someone who has come from heaven to personally guide us to God. A divine road map. Otherwise, we'll be as confused as I was, staring at a paper with nothing but a bunch of crisscross lines.

Principle

Jesus is our divine road map, leading us to the Father.

Ponder

- What's your initial reaction to Christ's claim that he is the only way to the Father?
- When have you found it helpful to know that Jesus is your divine road map?

Pursue: For a deeper dive, study John 14:4–12.

Lord God, thank you for sending Jesus, not only as my Saviour, but also as my road map to you, my heavenly Father.

"Remain in Me"

Our friends in Oregon owned a dog who chased his tail, over and over, until he was overcome by dizziness and passed out. When he recovered, the poor pup continued his pointless pursuit for hours. One day we visited them and didn't see their dog. They sadly shared that he had chased his tail in the middle of the street and, well, you can figure out the rest.

Silly dog. Imagine chasing after something you'll never catch. Spinning round and round until it wears you out, then takes you out. But like this foolish canine, we do the same thing—running in circles, caught up in life's hectic pace. We jump out of bed, grab some coffee, and dash off to work. We blitz through our day and come home worn out and burned out.

Jesus was aware of this danger. At the Last Supper, after warning his disciples he was going away, he shared a secret with them. "I am the vine; you are the branches. If you remain in me and I in you, you will bear much fruit; apart from me you can do nothing" (John 15:5). In light of his departure, what instruction could be more important than remaining in him?

A branch has one job: stay connected to the vine. It doesn't grunt and groan with white-knuckling labour to produce fruit. It simply remains connected to the life source. The vine draws nutrients and water from the soil, energy from the sun, and fruit happens. Eleven times in John 15:1–10, Jesus uses the word *remain*. He tells us to remain, remain, remain in him.

It's simple science. If we snip a branch from a vine, it dies. This detail was crucial for the disciples. Within a few hours, their master would be arrested, tried, and executed. They would need his abiding presence to get through that night and all the days that followed, until they breathed their final breath.

Remaining in Jesus isn't a tool to give us what we want in life—it is life. We soak in his presence continually. But apart from him? We can do nothing.

We have a choice. Remain in Jesus and experience life—real life—a life of fruitfulness. Or run around in circles, powered by our own effort. Apart from Christ, we're like a dog chasing its tail.

Principle

Remaining in Jesus brings the life he intends for us.

Ponder

- What most often tempts you to chase your tail?
- What spiritual practices can you adopt to help you remain in Jesus?

Pursue: For a deeper dive, study John 15:1–17.

Lord, I confess that I am easily pulled away by worldly pursuits and slip away from remaining connected to you. During those times, please bring me back to you.

Garden of the Oil Press

In ancient Israel, olive oil was crucial for daily life—used for cooking, medicine, cosmetics, and lighting, as well as religious rituals. Every village of any size contained an olive press, which often weighed several tons. Two huge stones were pressed together to crush the olives in a *gat shemanim*, the Hebrew phrase meaning "a place for pressing oils."

The night before he died, Jesus brought his disciples to Gethsemane—Garden of the Oil Press—to wait with him as he prayed. Jesus' admission to his disciples gives us some insight into his frame of mind: "My soul is overwhelmed with sorrow to the point of death" (Mark 14:34). "And being in anguish, he prayed more earnestly." How deep was his anguish? "And his sweat was like drops of blood falling to the ground" (Luke 22:44). Jesus literally sweat blood.

The setting for this scene is ironic. When olives were pressed in a gethsemane, oil poured forth. As our Saviour was pressed in the garden of Gethsemane, it wasn't oil that flowed, but blood intermingled with sweat. This is a rare medical phenomenon known as *hematidrosis*, defined as "a condition in which capillary blood vessels that feed the sweat glands rupture, causing them to exude blood, occurring under conditions of extreme physical or emotional stress."[2]

What caused this extreme emotional stress for Jesus? You and I. He took upon himself the weight of every sin ever committed by humanity. Every act of incest, murder, and treachery. Every lie and slanderous word weighed him down like a multi-tonne olive press. At times we say, "I'm carrying the weight of the world on my shoulders." This is a figure of speech, but it was literally true of Jesus. No one else in history has experienced this kind of pressure.

We all have our Gethsemane moments—those times in life when we feel as if a stone olive press is crushing us. As I write this, I'm experiencing stress so profound, I can hardly think. My wife is in her final days of Stage 4 cancer. More than once, I've cried out, "God, I can't handle this." But when I speak these words, the Lord brings me back to Gethsemane, where Jesus lay with his face in the dirt, tears running down his cheeks, his forehead dripping blood, and I realise he took upon himself the weight of the world. I know he understands how I feel—and so much more. This enables me to face another day, confident I can make it through.

Principle

Jesus' willingness to be crushed by the weight of our sin empowers me to face my own crushing trials.

Ponder

- When have you felt as if the weight of the world lay on your shoulders?
- How does knowing that Jesus faced pressure greater than anyone else has ever known help you face each day?

Pursue: For a deeper dive, study Luke 22:39–46.

Lord Jesus, in a tiny way, I can relate to your experience in Gethsemane. Thank you for taking my sin upon your shoulders. Help me look to you for strength when I face my own Gethsemane.

"Not My Will"

What do you consider the greatest prayer ever uttered? The Serenity Prayer, with its simplicity? The Lord's Prayer, in all its beauty? I think it's the prayer uttered by Jesus in the garden of Gethsemane. This prayer is more the Lord's prayer than the Lord's Prayer itself: "Not my will, but yours be done" (Luke 22:42).

As Jesus was on the verge of being arrested, he wrestled with the anguish that lay before him. In intense spiritual warfare, he pleaded with his Father, "If you are willing, take this cup from me" (Luke 22:42). Hebrews 5:7 tells us that Jesus begged God "with fervent cries and tears." But even as he pleaded with his Abba to spare his life, Jesus surrendered to his Father's will. He uttered that powerful phrase, "Not my will, but yours be done."

I find it easy to surrender to God's will as long as God does things *my* way—exactly as I think he should. But what about those times when my will doesn't match his? Perhaps God has a different plan for me than what I expect, or in some cases, want.

Saying these seven simple words, "not my will, but yours be done," can be agonizing. Releasing something, or someone, into God's hands, and *really* meaning it—if you've been there, you know how painful it can be. But Jesus endured the anguish. He went through hell so we could go to heaven.

I don't have to like the way God chooses to answer my prayers. I might wish he'd select a different route. In the garden, Jesus knew what lay ahead (John 18:4). In a few hours, he'd face betrayal, abandonment, injustice, ridicule, beatings, and crucifixion. He demonstrated profound character to face this night from hell and surrender his will to carry out God's purposes—to trust God and do what was best for others.

Here's the big question. Am I willing to surrender to God's will, as Jesus did, or do I reverse Christ's prayer, and cry, "Not *your* will, but *mine* be done"? When we fully surrender, God gives us a peace "which transcends all understanding" (Philippians 4:7).

In the end, Jesus got up, dusted himself off, wiped the tears from his cheeks and the blood from his brow, lifted his head, and set out to face the angry mob approaching him. He'd already won the battle because he was fully surrendered to his Father.

Principle

When we pray "your will be done," we experience God's peace.

Ponder

- When have you found yourself reversing the words of Jesus' prayer in your heart and saying, "Not your will, but mine be done"?
- How has God blessed you when you surrender your will to his?

Pursue: For a deeper dive, study Hebrews 5:7–10.

Loving Father, so many times I struggle to surrender to you. Please help me pray as Jesus did, "Not my will, but yours be done."

Who's in Charge?

Bruce Lee, the king of kung fu, had no equal among men. Standing toe-to-toe with not merely one villain but a gang of ten thugs, he could easily best them all. His moves were so lightning fast, they appeared invisible. Yet as masterful as he was, he never had to face Jesus. Jesus wasn't the king of kung fu. He is incomparably more: the King of Kings, the Almighty Creator, the Great I Am—just for starters. If anyone ever considered facing Jesus, it was game over.

Consider the mob sent to arrest him in the garden of Gethsemane. John described the scene. "Judas came to the garden, guiding a detachment of soldiers. . . . They were carrying torches, lanterns and weapons" (John 18:3). The Greek word translated "detachment" refers to a military cohort, consisting of three hundred to six hundred men.[3]

Three-hundred soldiers—trained killers—all sent to arrest one Galilean carpenter? Perhaps they suspected he was more than a mere carpenter. What follows in the text validates their numbers:

> Jesus, knowing all that was going to happen to him, went out and asked them, "Who is it you want?"
>
> "Jesus of Nazareth," they replied.
>
> "I am he," Jesus said. . . . When Jesus said, "I am he," they drew back and fell to the ground." (John 18:4–6)

In Greek, his literal words were, "I Am." Translators inserted *he* for a better flow in English. Jesus identifies himself as the Great I Am, the name God assigned to himself (Exodus 3:14).

Jesus merely uttered his name, and the detachment of soldiers fell to the ground. They didn't trip over each other in surprise. These were trained professional warriors. Jesus proved he was in charge—that by merely uttering his name as God incarnate, no human force could stop him. He didn't need to put any kung fu moves on them. Had he desired, he could have disintegrated the universe with one word.

Jesus was totally in control of the events surrounding his death. He was not murdered. He was not martyred. He willingly laid down his life as a sacrifice for all mankind. That night in the garden, Jesus was completely in charge.

The same is still true today. When a mob from the Enemy comes against us—whether it's depression, fear, doubt, anger, or any other circumstance over which we have no control—Jesus' power is as great today as two thousand years ago. He is the Great I Am—and he's still in charge.

Principle

Jesus is in charge of every situation.

Ponder

- When have you needed to know that Jesus is in charge of the universe?
- What circumstances are you currently facing in which you need to remember that Jesus is the Great I Am?

Pursue: For a deeper dive, study John 18:1–12.

Lord Jesus, you are the Great I Am. Forgive my times of doubt. Help me look to you for the power to face the mobs the Enemy brings against me.

Sweet Tea

My wife once owned a pet chicken. Yes, a pet chicken. A rooster to be exact. She named the bird "Sweet Tea," because in his chick-hood, her feathered friend sat on her lap atop a towel and drank from her iced tea glass. (I'm just glad he wasn't a vulture.) Several times I considered switching to the Food Channel to catch a glimpse of his future, but my better judgement prevailed.

One day Linda discovered some of his feathers on our road and couldn't locate Sweet Tea. She was distraught, afraid he'd been promoted to poultry paradise. Eventually, she found the rooster alive and well. He'd simply wandered off.

Unlike Sweet Tea, on the night before Christ's death, his disciples didn't accidentally wander off from Jesus. When a mob came to arrest him, Mark recounts what happened., "Then everyone deserted him and fled" (14:50). One simple statement, packed with volumes of emotion.

Imagine the rejection Jesus must have felt. Most of us have someone to turn to in times of crisis, but Jesus had no one. In his greatest hour of need, he stood alone, surrounded by a mob. Isaiah 53:3 states, "He was despised and abandoned by men" (NASB). His disciples may not have despised him, but they certainly abandoned him.

Add to this Isaiah's description, "We all, like sheep [or chickens], have gone astray" (53:6). Wandering astray probably poses a greater danger than abandoning Jesus because, like Sweet Tea, we don't even realise it's happening. Most of us aren't going to jump out of bed tomorrow and say, "I think I'll abandon Jesus today," and then head out on a sinning spree like the Prodigal Son (Luke 15:11–32). But slowly slipping away from our passion for Jesus? We don't even realise when we've wandered into the land of spiritual lethargy. We're not cold towards Jesus. We're simply lukewarm. Dull and discouraged.

The writer of Hebrews warns, "We must pay the most careful attention, therefore, to what we have heard, so that we do not drift away" (2:1). Like a boat adrift on the sea, we can end up far from where we intended.

What's the solution? Pursue the Lord, press into Jesus, live perpetually in his presence. Every day. It's not easy in a world of distractions. But it's critical for our spiritual survival. Fleeing from Jesus or merely meandering off—both can be deadly.

Principle

Wandering away from our Lord probably poses a greater threat than abandoning him.

Ponder

- What spiritual practices might help prevent you from unintentionally wandering away from Jesus?
- What changes might you need to make to remain more closely connected to the Lord throughout the day?

Pursue: For a deeper dive, study Hebrews 2:1–4.

> *Lord, remind me that I am "prone to wander" as the hymn says. Draw me closer to your heart each and every day.*[4]

A Faithful Friend

In August 1936, a sheepherder in Fort Benton, Montana, fell ill and died. His body was placed on a train heading east. There was no funeral, and no one came to say goodbye, except for one faithful friend. He watched silently as the locomotive disappeared over the horizon. His friend returned to the train depot the next day, and the next, and the next. Every day for nearly six years the sheepherder's friend came to the depot and stared at the spot where he had said goodbye.

No one remembers the name of the sheepherder, but everyone around Fort Benton knows the name of his friend: Shep the sheepdog. Today a bronze statue of Shep stands in Fort Benton's town square, honouring its most famous citizen—a tribute to a faithful friend's devotion.[5]

Jesus needed a friend like Shep on the night he was arrested. His friends scattered as if running from a lighted stick of dynamite. Eventually, Peter followed at a distance (Luke 22:54), where he observed Jesus' trial in the courtyard of the high priest. As he waited, a servant girl recognised him as one of Christ's followers, but Peter denied even knowing Jesus. Another servant identified him, and once again Peter denied Jesus. When someone recognised him a third time as a follower of Jesus, "Peter replied, 'Man, I don't know what you're talking about!' As he was speaking, the rooster crowed. The Lord turned and looked straight at Peter" (vv. 60–61). Imagine the emotions displayed on the Lord's face. Imagine the agony in Peter's heart. "And he went outside and wept bitterly" (v. 62).

Peter's not alone in denying Jesus. We're all guilty. Whenever we shrink from speaking boldly about him, whenever we loosen our standards around unbelievers, whenever we cave into peer pressure or yield to our flesh, we deny Jesus.

When we do, we can't allow Satan to overwhelm us with shame. When Peter repented, Jesus restored him and gave him the privilege of preaching the first gospel sermon (Acts 2). No matter how often we deny Jesus, his grace and willingness to restore us is more than sufficient. He will never deny us.

Shep the sheepdog provides us a wonderful model of friendship. Instead of denying Jesus or forgetting him, let's remain his faithful friend.

Principle

Rather than denying Jesus, let's strive to be his friend.

Ponder

- Under what circumstances are you most susceptible to denying Jesus?
- How can you be a better friend to Jesus?

Pursue: For a deeper dive, study Luke 22:54–62.

Dearest Jesus, forgive me for those times when I behave like Peter and act as if I'm ashamed of you. Show me how, especially in times of trial, I can be a better friend to you.

To This You Were Called

Any eating establishment featuring a giant rodent as its main attraction might expect trouble. In 2013, at a Chuck E. Cheese restaurant near Chicago, a brawl erupted, resulting in two arrests. More than thirty people joined in the scuffle, injuring three adults. Fortunately, no children were hurt. Evidently, the fighting began over a dispute regarding game prize tickets.[6]

I've enjoyed numerous kids' parties with the rat at Chuck E. Cheese. But fighting over game tickets? Ever seen the quality of the prizes? They aren't exactly Neiman-Marcus-calibre gifts.

Bizarre situations can cause us to lose our temper, especially if we feel we've been treated unjustly. If anyone had the right to strike back at others, it was Jesus. On the last night of his life, he was mocked, beaten, and spit upon, yet he didn't retaliate.

Peter describes our calling and Christ's restraint, "To this you were called, because Christ suffered for you, leaving you an example, that you should follow in his steps. 'He committed no sin, and no deceit was found in his mouth.' When they hurled their insults at him, he did not retaliate; when he suffered, he made no threats. Instead, he entrusted himself to him who judges justly" (1 Peter 2:21–23).

At any moment, Jesus could have ended his suffering. He had the power to call down thousands of angels and return to heaven (Matthew 26:53). One word from him, and his torturers would have instantly been incinerated. Yet he refrained. Consider something even more amazing: Jesus endured this monumental suffering to bring salvation to the very ones who tortured him.

How could he withstand such torment without retaliating? Peter explains, "He entrusted himself" to the Father (1 Peter 2:23). Jesus surrendered his will to his Father. But here's the tough part. Jesus calls us to imitate him. Like Christ, we are called to bear unjust suffering (vv. 19–20). I don't like this. I don't want to be called to suffer unjustly. But following our Master requires it.

When we feel mistreated, let's come back to Christ's example. Any ill treatment we receive will never compare to his suffering. Let's take our eyes off any injustice others inflict on us and focus on Jesus. Even when we're denied justice, he will give us the strength to entrust ourselves to God the Father, who judges justly.

Principle

When we face injustice, focus on Jesus, who entrusted himself to his Father.

Ponder

- When have you been called upon to suffer unjustly?
- How might focusing on Jesus help you in such situations?

Pursue: For a deeper dive, study 1 Peter 2:13–24

*Lord Jesus, you are amazing. I worship you for the
way you modelled the right response to unjust suffering.
Give me the strength to follow your example.*

A Cowardly Judge

Imagine standing before a judge who hears your case. At the end of the proceedings, he declares you "not guilty." But the gallery shouts their disapproval, so the judge reverses his decision and states, "Bailiff, lead the defendant away to be executed." This would be insane. A judge pronouncing a defendant "not guilty" and then executing him? This could never happen.

But it did. The judge was Pontius Pilate, and the defendant, Jesus of Nazareth.

As Jesus' night from hell wound down, the Jewish council met at sunrise and officially brought an indictment of death against him. Then they dragged him before Pilate, the Roman prefect. Because the Romans ruled the Jews, only the prefect could issue an edict in capital crimes.

Immediately the Jews changed the charges against Jesus from blasphemy (Matthew 26:65) to treason (Luke 23:2). The crime of blasphemy would have carried no weight with Pilate, but treason was a capital offence. Pilate recognised Jesus' innocence and observed "it was out of self-interest that [the Jews] had handed Jesus over to him" (Matthew 27:18).

Pilate hoped a good beating would satisfy the Jews, so he "had him flogged" (John 19:1)—a simple word describing one of the most brutal forms of torture in history. A prisoner was stripped naked and his hands tied to a post. Two soldiers beat him with a whip containing pieces of bone and metal. The skin on his back was shredded. But even after seeing Jesus as a bloody mess, the Jews shouted even louder, "Crucify! Crucify!" (John 19:6).

Pilate then declared, "I find no basis for a charge against him" (John

19:6), pronouncing Jesus "not guilty." But finally, "Pilate handed him over to them to be crucified" (v. 16). From "not guilty" to "execute him," almost in the same breath.

Pilate was a coward. He was torn between whatever convictions he had against executing an innocent man and his desire to please the populace. As a politician, he couldn't afford to go against the will of the people—especially in this case. The Jews might incite a riot or report him to Caesar, who could remove him from his post.

This was one more layer of injustice in Christ's suffering. Satan must have been delighted as the punishment was piled on Jesus. But even in these unjust circumstances, God was at work, using a cowardly magistrate to fulfil his eternal purpose so Jesus would be crucified and save humanity.

Principle

Besides all the other suffering of Jesus, he was declared "not guilty," then sentenced to die.

Ponder

- What emotions arise as you consider all the injustice Jesus suffered?
- When has God used your suffering to fulfil his purpose in your life?

Pursue: For a deeper dive, study John 19:1–16.

Loving Saviour, as much as my heart breaks when I think of what you endured, I'm so grateful that you willingly endured such harsh treatment so I could be saved.

Treated Like a Common Criminal

S ally, a woman who is the epitome of fashion and elegance, found herself falsely accused of shoplifting at an upscale clothing shop. She purchased an expensive blouse, and as she exited the shop, alarms went off, and security forces pounced on her. The shop clerk had forgotten to remove the plastic security device. "How horrible for you!" cried her sympathetic friends as she shared the story. "It must have been so distressing for you."

"Oh, it wasn't any trouble," said Sally. "I was able to explain who I was and what happened. No, the really bad part was the feeling of being treated like a common criminal!"[7]

Treated like a common criminal? If you're innocent, this would be disturbing. But the story of Christ's death is unimaginably worse. The only sinless, perfect person ever to live was treated *worse* than a common criminal. After being arrested, he was dragged through six trials. Then he was mocked, beaten, and spit upon—twice. Mark describes the scene. "Then some began to spit at him; they blindfolded him, struck him with his fists, and said, 'Prophesy!' And the guards took him and beat him" (14:65). Imagine—these were members of the Jewish high council. Then, this deplorable behaviour was repeated. Pilate's Roman guards not only beat Jesus but also placed a crown of thorns and a purple robe on him, then bowed in mock worship (15:16–20).

Mocking him as a fake prophet and a clown king was uncalled for. Even worse, Mark's narrative adds one short word: "spit" (14:65). Spitting in a person's face is a despicable act intended for one purpose:

humiliation. The sinless Son of God suffered mistreatment far worse than even a rabid dog deserves. Jesus suffered every form of abuse imaginable during that night from hell, was condemned by a cowardly judge, and then nailed to a cross.

As we end this section, meditate on the events leading up to the crucifixion. As much as possible, join in Jesus' suffering and humiliation. Imagine how it felt for the pure and perfect Son of God, who came to save mankind, to be treated worse than a common criminal.

Principle

Jesus was treated worse than a common criminal.

Ponder

- As you meditate on this aspect of Christ's suffering, what thoughts and feelings arise?
- How can you show Jesus your gratitude for enduring this unjust treatment to save you?

Pursue: For a deeper dive, study Mark 14:64–65 and 15:16–20.

Lord Jesus, I bow at your feet. Unlike the soldiers who mocked you, I worship you as the Almighty Son of God.

PART FOUR

The Cross

God could quite justly have abandoned us to our fate. He could have left us alone to reap the fruit of our wrongdoing and to perish in our sins. It is what we deserved. But he did not. Because he loved us, he came after us in Christ. He pursued us even to the desolate anguish of the cross, where he bore our sins, guilt, judgement and death. It takes a hard and stony heart to remain unmoved by love like that.

John Stott[1]

Pure Sacrificial Love

The greatest week of my life was my first trip to Israel. The greatest experience of my greatest week was walking the Via Dolorosa, the Way of Sorrow—the route tradition tells us Jesus took, carrying his cross to Calvary. I was overcome with emotion, and tears ran down my cheeks. I glanced at Linda. She was wiping her eyes as well.

After Pilate sentenced Jesus, he took his cross and headed up the hill to be crucified. He knew, in his weakened condition, he'd stumble and fall. He knew the mockery was only beginning.

He knew the soldiers would drive spikes into his hands and feet. He knew he'd hang in misery for hours.

But knowing all this, Jesus thought of others first. A group of women were weeping for him. Jesus paused and said, "Do not weep for me; weep for yourselves and for your children" (Luke 23:28). Jesus then warned them of the destruction of Jerusalem forty years later. At the worst moment of his life, Jesus was thinking of others. Such pure sacrificial love.

As the cross dropped into the ground, Jesus looked down and saw seething, hate-filled faces cursing him. He looked to heaven and prayed for the very ones who were killing him, "Father, forgive them, for they do not know what they are doing" (v. 34). Such pure sacrificial love.

Two thieves were crucified with Christ. Hanging there, one of them requested, "Jesus, remember me when you come into your kingdom." Jesus answered, "Today you will be with me in paradise" (vv. 42–43). Even as he was dying a torturous death, Jesus was concerned for this criminal.

Is there any wonder the centurion in charge of the crucifixion exclaimed, "Surely he was the Son of God!" (Matthew 27:54). This soldier had probably supervised many crucifixions, but he had never witnessed anything close to such pure sacrificial love.

I don't know how to process this. How do we wrap our minds around this kind of love? It strips away our pride, our excuses, our sense of self-importance. It forces us to grasp our desperate need for God to save us from ourselves. There's no historical parallel to this singular demonstration of selflessness. Every act of bravery, every other sacrificial deed pales in comparison. We can only praise Jesus, receive his gift, and extend his pure sacrificial love to others.

Principle

Jesus' sacrificial love has no equal in history.

Ponder

- When and how have you experienced Christ's sacrificial love?
- How can you demonstrate sacrificial love for someone?

Pursue: For a deeper dive, study Luke 23:26–47.

Dear Jesus, I am awestruck as I consider your sacrificial love. Thank you for giving your life for me. Forgive me for the times when I place my needs ahead of others'.

Excruciating

Psychotherapist Richard Bandler tells the story of visiting a patient in a mental institution who insisted he was Jesus. Bandler left, then returned and measured the man's arms and height. Next, he brought in a hammer, nails, and lumber. "What are you doing?" the man asked.

Richard answered, "Are you Jesus?"

The man replied, "Yes, my son."

"Then you know why I'm here," Bandler said.

Suddenly the man recalled his true identity. "I'm not Jesus! I'm not Jesus!" he yelled. Doctors closed the case on this would-be Messiah.[2]

One word sums up the reason any sane person would resist being nailed to a cross: *excruciating*. In fact, the English word *excruciating* comes from a Latin term meaning "out of the cross." The Roman statesman Cicero stated that the word *cross* should never be mentioned in polite society. He added, "[Let] the very word 'cross' . . . be far removed from not only the bodies of Roman citizens, but even from their thoughts, their eyes, and their ears."[3]

No other form of death could match it. As Jesus' friends and family watched, a soldier grabbed his arm, stretched it over the crossbeam, and drove a spike into his wrist, crushing bone, muscle, and tendons. He repeated the process with the other arm. After fitting the crossbeam to the upright post and nailing down Jesus' feet, guards dropped the cross, with its prisoner attached, into a hole with a thud.

The pressure on Jesus' chest from being suspended from his arms made it impossible for him to breathe. To compensate, he had to straighten his legs. Unable to withstand the pressure on his lungs, Jesus would push himself up, putting his weight on his legs and scraping his recently flogged back on the rough wood of the cross. When the pain in his feet became too intense, he'd drop back down. He did this over and over again, prolonging his torture, as he hung on the cross for six hours.

Jesus' muscles cramped and convulsed. His open wounds attracted insects and birds. He refused to take wine mixed with myrrh, a common pain killer, probably to remain alert (Mark 15:23).

After hearing this story dozens of times, we may grow numb to the torturous suffering Jesus endured—or to his love. As indescribable as his pain was, his love was greater. Jesus endured this anguish for the joy set before him (Hebrews 12:2). You and I mean more to him than anything else. Even in the midst of excruciating pain.

Principle

Jesus endured the excruciating pain of the cross for each of us.

Ponder

- As uncomfortable as it is, how does focusing on Jesus' pain on the cross encourage and inspire you?
- How can you show Jesus your deep appreciation for his sacrifice?

Pursue: For a deeper dive, study Mark 15:21–39.

Precious Jesus, my heart breaks as I read of your suffering, especially knowing it was my sins that caused your pain. Thank you for your sacrifice. Once again, I surrender my life to you.

"Father, Forgive Them"

In 2012, Carl Ericsson, a seventy-three-year-old South Dakota man, was sentenced to life imprisonment for murdering a former high school classmate. Ericsson nursed a grudge for over fifty years against Norman Johnson, a star athlete in high school, who had pulled a jock strap over Ericsson's head. The resentment over this locker-room bullying grew until one day, Ericsson rang Johnson's doorbell and shot him dead.[4]

Forgiving others can be one of the most challenging commands in Scripture. Our flesh protests, "It's not fair! I have the right to get even." But Jesus modelled a different way.

Hanging on the cross, Jesus had been wronged in every way possible. Illegally arrested, unlawfully tried, ridiculed, beaten, spit upon, flogged. To top it off, he was the only sinless person ever to live. Yet hearing the mockery of those for whom he was dying, he didn't call for God to smite them with lightning. His first recorded words on the cross were, "Father, forgive them, for they do not know what they are doing" (Luke 23:34).

We've probably all suffered deep personal injustice. Perhaps we've fantasized about getting even. But if *anyone* had the right to take revenge, it was Jesus. Instead, he showed us how to forgive. Jesus taught, "But if you do not forgive others their sins, your Father will not forgive your sins" (Matthew 6:15). Here's why: God knows that refusing to forgive will destroy us, as Carl Ericsson's story demonstrates. As the old saying goes, it's like drinking poison and waiting for the other person to die. An unforgiving heart hurts only us. Forgiveness frees us.

Forgiving doesn't mean we feel okay about the one who wronged us. Forgiveness isn't a feeling, it's a decision. We choose to entrust the person and event to God and let him dispense justice. "Do not take revenge, my dear friends, but leave room for God's wrath, for it is written: 'It is mine to avenge; I will repay,' says the Lord" (Romans 12:19).

Don't worry. God will take care of it. Once we consciously choose to forgive, God goes to work on healing us. It might take time, but we can trust God with the injustice.

When we're hurting from the pain, we can look to Jesus as our example. No matter how badly we've been wronged, we'll never suffer as much as he did. Yet amid deep agony, he prayed, "Father, forgive them."

Principle

Jesus showed us how to forgive when he prayed, "Father, forgive them."

Ponder

- What personal injustices have you struggled with in the past, and how did you move past them?
- How does focusing on the example of Jesus help you forgive others?

Pursue: For a deeper dive, study Matthew 18:21–35.

Jesus, I know you want me to be free, but sometimes it's so hard to forgive others. Please give me your power to forgive my wrongdoers, just as you did on the cross.

"Today You Will Be with Me"

Two men missed their flight at an airport. One was a minute late. The other missed it by an hour. Can you imagine the man who barely missed it laughing at the other man and saying, "I was only a minute late, but you missed it by an hour." This is almost impossible to imagine. Either way, they both missed their flights.

Similarly, we've all missed our flight on Heavenly Airways. No matter how good we think we are, we fall short. The apostle Paul declared, "There is no one righteousness, not even one" (Romans 3:10). Our only hope for heaven is God's gift of eternal life. He purchased our ticket at the cross, along with another unlikely passenger's.

Two criminals were crucified with Jesus. One of them "hurled insults at him" (Luke 23:39). The other rebuked his companion. "Don't you fear God . . . ? We are punished justly. . . . But this man has done nothing wrong" (Luke 23:40–41). His concern for another dying criminal must have turned heads in the crowd.

Then he added, "Jesus, remember me when you come into your kingdom" (v. 42). The man didn't ask for much—no prominent position, not even an entrance pass. Just to be remembered.

Then, with one divine message, Jesus gives him the trip of a lifetime. "Today you will be with me in paradise" (v. 43). These words changed his eternal destiny. The criminal still suffered. He still bled. He still died a horrible death. But he died with hope in his heart—hope that couldn't be extinguished, even on a cross. While others saw him as a scumbag, Jesus saw him as his precious creation who'd been deceived by the Enemy.

This thief isn't so different from the rest of us. Do you suppose he planned to grow up to be a thief? On Career Day at school, did he tell his classmates, "I wanna be a thief and die a torturous death"? What happened? Somehow life turned out different than he planned. No one plans to become an addict or be convicted of a crime, but we all yield to sin and experience failure in life.

We've all missed our flight on Heavenly Airways. But God has different travel arrangements prepared for us. He offers us a second chance on Forgiven Flights—just like the thief on the cross. What must we do? Simply accept the ticket. It doesn't matter how late we are—a minute or an hour—we'll always make that flight.

Principle

Jesus offers us all a second chance.

Ponder

- When have you felt disillusioned with life?
- How is your life like the repentant thief's?

Pursue: For a deeper dive, study Luke 23:32–43.

Christ Jesus, I acknowledge you as my Saviour. Like the thief, only through your grace and forgiveness do I have any hope of eternal life. Thank you for second chances.

The Personal Nature of the Cross

As he hung on the cross, Jesus looked down at those standing below. Two faces caught his eye. One was the first face he ever saw. Standing near her was his best friend. How it must have ripped his heart, seeing his mother watch him die. He looked at Mary and said to her, "Here is your son." Then, turning his gaze to John, he said, "Here is your mother" (John 19:26–27). One of his last dying acts was to commit his mother to John's care and provide for her as her oldest son. Jesus wasn't only the Son of God. He was also the son of Mary. He was a man who loved and cared for his mother, even as he was dying. The cross was deeply personal for Jesus.

The cross is personal for us as well. We may be able to conceive of Jesus dying for a mass of humanity, like ants in a colony, scurrying everywhere. Out of billions of people, I'm just a speck. But not to Jesus. His sacrifice was personal. Jesus didn't give his life for a bunch of nameless, faceless humans. He died for each of us individually.

My sin crucified Jesus. My sin compelled him to leave heaven, put on flesh, be tortured, and ultimately be nailed to a cross. But there's beauty in this reality. Even if I'd been the only person who ever sinned, Jesus would have died for me. Paul certainly thought so. In Galatians 2:20 he wrote, "The life I now live in the body, I live by faith in the Son of God, who loved me and gave himself for me."

Notice how personal the cross was to Paul. He didn't say, "Jesus loved all of humanity and died for everyone," although this is true.

From Paul's perspective, Jesus died for him personally. Likewise, Jesus died for you, as if you were the only sinner on earth.

We live in an impersonal world, where we're regarded as a number: Social Security, driver's licence, credit cards. But not with Jesus. Before the creation of the world, he saw us, he knew us, he loved us, and he died for us—individually. Never forget this. The cross is personal for us all.

Principle

The cross is deeply personal, for Jesus and for each of us.

Ponder

- What emotions arise as you ponder the fact that Jesus would have died for you even if you were the only person who ever sinned?
- How will you respond to the truth that you are so deeply loved by God?

Pursue: For a deeper dive, study John 19:25–27.

Precious Jesus, thank you, thank you, thank you for dying for me personally. Help me live in this reality, knowing I am so deeply loved by you.

"It Is Finished"

The final words of famous people can be revealing. Consider these: "Money can't buy life" (Bob Marley). "All my possessions for a moment of time!" (Queen Elizabeth I). "I'm bored with it all" (Winston Churchill).[5]

Shortly before Jesus died, he uttered three short words. "It is finished" (John 19:30). Nothing complex or poetic. But these three short words altered humankind's history forever. What did Jesus mean? What was finished when he died?

In the Old Testament, when the high priest offered a sacrifice for the sins of the people on the Day of Atonement, all their transgressions were figuratively placed on a lamb. The priest would emerge and declare to the waiting crowd, "It is finished." This was merely a shadow of the literal, perfect sacrifice offered by the Lamb of God (Hebrews 10:1–5). By uttering, "It is finished," Jesus declared that the need for animal sacrifices had ended.[6]

But there's more. In New Testament times, when a craftsman completed a project, an artist finished his work, or a loan was paid in full, the identical words were used: "It is finished." This phrase was familiar to those standing at the cross.[7]

All the richness of this expression converges at the cross. On multiple levels, Jesus left no doubt that his work on earth was complete. He was born to die. The last few of the more than three hundred messianic prophecies were fulfilled. And, most importantly, his work of salvation was finished on the cross.

There's nothing we can add to or take from what Jesus did at Calvary. Jesus made this clear with his dying breath. Of course, we must respond to God's offer of salvation. But eternal life is not *based* on human effort—trying harder, doing more, being better—because we can never be good enough to cleanse ourselves of even one sin. None of us has enough spiritual oomph to pull ourselves up by our bootstraps. We *all* need a Saviour.

Our walk with Jesus isn't a self-improvement plan. It's a Christ-dependent plan. When Jesus uttered his dying words, "It is finished," it *was* finished! *Is* finished. Forever. His blood covers every sin ever committed by every person—past, present, and future.

We're all hopelessly and helplessly lost without Jesus. This is why his three dying words are so earth-shattering—literally. An earthquake followed this short declaration.

We can rest in his finished work on the cross. We can breathe an eternal sigh of relief, because our salvation is secure. It is finished.

Principle

When Jesus said, "It is finished," he completed his work of salvation on the cross.

Ponder

- On a scale of one to ten, how much do you struggle with accepting that your salvation was completed on the cross and not through any effort of your own?
- Why do you think people cling so strongly to "try harder" religion?

Pursue: For a deeper dive, study Hebrews 10:1–18.

Jesus, thank you for your completed work on the cross. Thank you for paying the price for my sins. Help me rest in this reality.

Darkness during Daylight

Sunday, May 18, 1980, near Coeur d'Alene, Idaho. I'd just returned from church and was weeding a flower bed. Glancing to the west, I observed a pitch-black cloud approaching. I yelled to our neighbour, "There's a huge storm coming."

Shaking his head, he replied, "No. Mount St. Helens exploded this morning." Although two hundred miles away, because of wind direction, we were in the path of the smoke and ashfall. As the sky grew dark, I had the bizarre feeling of midnight at midday. Streetlights came on and our chickens roosted. An hour later, grey volcanic ash began raining on us, accompanied by a surreal tinkling sound. It covered the ground in an inch-thick shroud and filled me with an eerie awe.

How do you suppose those who experienced the darkness at the cross would have described it? Eerie? Surreal? Reverential? Matthew 27:45 simply states, "From noon until three in the afternoon darkness came over all the land"—as if God's finger reached down and blotted out the sun for three hours, when it should have been brightest.

I wonder how many passersby realised, at some level, the devastating disaster that was occurring? God paid us a visit from heaven . . . and we killed him. It doesn't get any worse than that. Nothing but a midnight-like darkness would be fitting. A darkness much more awe-inspiring than volcanic ashfall. A darkness that could be felt in the depths of the human soul—physical, yes, but a mere reflection of what was occurring in the spiritual realm.

My guess is more than a few standing there uttered the first-century equivalent of "Oh no! What on earth have we done?" Perhaps this is partly why the centurion declared, "Surely [Jesus] was the Son of God!" (Matthew 27:54).

This darkness was Satan's brightest moment as he frolicked in the delight of watching Christ die. But only for a moment. Because when Jesus uttered the words, "Into your hands I commit my spirit," Jesus died (Luke 23:46). At that instant—during the darkest hour in human history—Jesus delivered us from the bondage of eternal darkness and filled us with his light.

Man's darkest hour—killing the Son of God—ushered in mankind's brightest moment, our eternal salvation. Only God could take the worst event ever and turn it into the greatest blessing. And he promises to do this in your life (Romans 8:28). Remember this truth when you're immersed in darkness. Your brightest moment might be only moments away.

Principle

Man's darkest hour ushered in mankind's brightest moment.

Ponder

- Had you been one of the people responsible for killing Jesus, how would you have felt standing there in the darkness?
- When have you experienced an extremely dark time that ushered in one of your brightest moments?

Pursue: For a deeper dive, study Matthew 27:50–56.

Lord God, I praise you for the amazing way you work.
You took the worst event in human history and used
it to produce our greatest blessing, eternal life.

Access to God's Office

A young boy walked through a corridor in the White House. He manoeuvred past the guards and made his way into the Oval Office, where the president of the United States was immersed in official paperwork. Without a moment's hesitation, this boy sashayed right up to the desk of the most powerful man in the world, crawled under it, and began playing.

Neither the president nor anyone else was surprised by his actions, for one simple reason. The president was John F. Kennedy, and the young boy was his son, John F. Kennedy Jr. Had any of us attempted to dash into the Oval Office unannounced, we would have been instantly shot. What made the difference? Relationship. To John-John, this man wasn't the president. He was Daddy.[8]

In the same way, we have access to God's office. Matthew informs us that, when Jesus died, "at that moment the curtain of the temple was torn in two from top to bottom" (27:51). That curtain was the barrier separating the Holy Place from the Holy of Holies, which represented God's presence on earth. The curtain was sixty feet high, thirty feet wide, and several inches thick and required three hundred priests to move it.[9] At the precise moment of Christ's death, it was torn from top to bottom, as if God reached down from heaven and ripped it in two, opening the way into his throne room.

The implications of this act are profound. Almighty God gives us open access into his office. He issues the invitation to "approach God's throne of grace with confidence, so that we may receive mercy and find grace to help us in our time of need" (Hebrews 4:16).

Too often we allow the Enemy to fill us with shame and convince us we're not worthy to approach God—that we've done too many bad things. Yet because the cross cleansed us of our sin, God reached down and tore the veil which separated us, removing our terror of the Almighty. Certainly, we approach God in humility, as Lord Most High. But he assures us that because Jesus removed the barrier between us and God at the cross, we can, as young John-John did, come confidently into his presence in time of need. For God's children, he's not merely King of Kings, he's our Daddy.

Principle

When Jesus died, the barrier between us and God was removed.

Ponder

- At what times are you most hesitant to come confidently into God's presence?
- How does understanding the picture of the torn curtain help?

Pursue: For a deeper dive, study Hebrews 4:12–16.

Abba Father, thank you for opening the way for me to come boldly before you with any request. Help me not be intimidated but to trust in your promise of forgiveness.

The Headless Snake

A missionary couple stepped into their kitchen and encountered an enormous snake—much longer than a man—that had slithered into their home. Terrified, they fled their house and found a neighbour who cut off the snake's head with a machete. Assuring the family that the snake was dead, he informed them it would continue moving and twitching until its nervous system stopped functioning. It would take time for the snake's body to realise it was dead. For several hours, the family waited while the snake thrashed about, smashing furniture and flailing against walls and windows, wreaking havoc, until its body understood it had no head.[10]

As Adam and Eve were banished from Eden, God spoke these words to the serpent, Satan: "I will put enmity between you and the woman, and between your offspring and hers; he will crush your head, and you will strike his heel" (Genesis 3:15). In this most ancient prophecy in Scripture, God gives us a glimpse of the cross. Satan bruised Christ's heel by inflicting physical injury on him. But Christ crushed Satan's head by forever destroying his power. Hebrews 2:14–15 explains, "[Christ] too shared in their humanity so that by his death he might break the power of him who holds the power of death—that is, the devil—and free those who all their lives were held in slavery by their fear of death."

Rather than living in victory, many believers cower in the shadows, fearing that Satan can harm us. Yes, Satan can still afflict us. Like the snake in the story, his head is crushed, but he can make life miserable for us. But because Jesus crushed his head on the cross, his power is only temporary. His ultimate power over us is gone. Guess how often the Bible tells us to fear the devil? Never. In fact, we now have power over him.

Like the snake in the missionaries' home, Satan is thrashing about, headless, but still wreaking havoc in our world. The family waited outside, knowing the snake was dead and that shortly they would return to their home. Likewise, we wait through this season of trouble, realising that our Enemy has been destroyed by the power of the cross. Soon, we'll return home. In the meantime, he can still inflict damage. But when Jesus bowed his head and died, Satan's power was forever destroyed. Walk in the victory of Jesus, knowing the serpent is headless.

Principle

We have nothing to fear from Satan because Jesus crushed his head at the cross.

Ponder

- In what situations do you find yourself succumbing to the fear of the Enemy?
- How does knowing that Jesus has crushed Satan open doors for you to live in freedom?

Pursue: For a deeper dive, study Genesis 3.

Lord God, during times of weakness, remind me that I have nothing to fear from the Enemy because his power has been destroyed forever.

Love Wounds

When my granddaughter, Olive, was six, she was warming up green beans on our stove under my supervision. When I stepped away momentarily, she leaned a bit too close and poof! Her dress erupted into flames. She screamed, and I quickly patted out the fire with my hands. I burned my palm in the process, but thankfully Olive was uninjured. I learned a critical lesson: Don't leave a child near an open flame. (Duh!) A few seconds longer and her hair could have caught fire. My quick action might have saved her life.

For several hours, I nursed my burned hand, clutching ice and dousing it with aloe vera. Then I witnessed a fascinating phenomenon. A large blister formed on my palm in the shape of a Valentine heart. I showed it to Olive, but in typical six-year-old style, she nodded, unimpressed, and skipped off on her merry way. Despite her less-than-grateful re-action, I'd risk injury again in a heartbeat and willingly endure pain to prevent her from suffering.

Isn't this what Jesus did for us? He put out the fire in our lives. "He took up our pain and bore our suffering. . . . He was pierced for our transgressions" (Isaiah 53:4–5). In the process, he acquired love wounds. His wound wasn't one measly blister but huge spike-sized holes in each hand and foot. He was willing to take the heat for us, paying our penalty, by enduring the most painful form of death known to the ancient world. Without hesitation, he'd do it again. He endured the cross "for the joy set before him" (Hebrews 12:2). To Jesus, it was an honour to die for us. In a tiny way, I can relate. I was honoured to bear love wounds that saved my granddaughter.

How many times do we react to Jesus' sacrifice in the same ho-hum way Olive did? She wasn't heartless. She was a six-year-old kid who didn't really grasp what I had done for her. So it is with us. We thank Jesus for what he did, then skip off on our merry way, moving on to what we may consider more important matters—watching sports or perusing social media. We grow numb to the love wounds Christ acquired for us. We've heard the story so often we forget its impact. It's critical to take time each day to pause and thank Jesus for his love wounds.

Principle

Jesus willingly acquired love wounds by absorbing our pain.

Ponder

- In what ways can you learn to be more grateful for the love wounds Jesus endured for you?
- How can you avoid growing numb to his great sacrifice?

Pursue: For a deeper dive, study Isaiah 53.

Lord Jesus, thank you for the love wounds you acquired for my benefit on the cross.

Do It Yourself

I've always been jealous of do-it-yourself handyman types—the kind of guys who can fix a carburettor with bailing wire and duct tape. My handyman efforts result in something that resembles a Tim Burton nightmare. Even as a child, I struggled in this area. My friends were into building model cars, so I decided I was into model cars. Only mine didn't quite have the pristine appearance of someone who knew what he was doing. Important parts were missing, and globs of glue surfaced in prominent places. My models looked like Demolition Derby rejects.

The same is true when it comes to our spiritual life. Do-it-yourself righteousness simply doesn't cut it. In Philippians 3:9, Paul speaks of "not having a righteousness of my own that comes from the law, but that which is through faith in Christ." He often testified of his experience as an over-the-top religious fanatic who not only exerted gargantuan effort to follow every ordinance of God but also specialized in keeping rules God hadn't even commanded. He was the quintessential rule-keeping dude (Philippians 3:4–6).

Maybe he thought he was close to keeping every law. Except for one teeny, tiny fact. He hated Jesus, God's promised Messiah, and attempted to obliterate his followers and his name from the face of the earth. But then Jesus knocked him to the ground on the road to Damascus, and it was game over. Paul surrendered his life to Christ. This moral do-it-yourselfer realised he needed a Saviour.

No matter how we see ourselves—as righteous as Paul or as wicked as Hitler—we *all* need saving. This is why Jesus left heaven. This is why he was born as a baby. This is why he lived a perfect life. And this is why he sacrificed himself on a hill outside Jerusalem—to pay for every sin every human would ever commit. Because our do-it-yourself righteousness is like trying to pay off the national debt with change from a piggy bank.

"Try harder" religion doesn't work. It leaves us frustrated—even neurotic—because no matter how hard we try, we can always try a little harder. This is why we need the cross. When we trust Jesus for our salvation, like Paul did, a huge burden rises off our shoulders. We can rest in Jesus and trust in his perfect righteousness. And for folks like me who can't even build a decent model car, this is really good news.

Principle

We need a Saviour because do-it-yourself-righteousness doesn't work.

Ponder

- When have you tried to accomplish something on your own and realised you needed serious help?
- What experiences have you had with do-it-yourself religion?

Pursue: For a deeper dive, study Philippians 3:1–14.

> *Great God, I know that I'm incapable of keeping your laws perfectly. Sometimes the harder I try, the more I fail. Thank you for sending a Saviour, Jesus.*

Eggy-Weggy

One afternoon I volunteered to pick up two of my grandchildren from school. I dragged along their three-year-old brother, Olin, who all day long had been toting a worthless plastic toy, which he affectionately dubbed "Eggy-Weggy." I strapped Olin into his car seat and drove to the school. That's when a tragedy of immense proportion occurred—he dropped Eggy-Weggy. Every two seconds, Olin wailed inconsolably, "Eggy-Weggy." When we arrived at the school, his brother Liam rescued Eggy-Weggy from the floorboard of my truck, and peace was restored to the galaxy.

Sighing in relief, I thought, how ridiculous it was for Olin to get so worked up over a worthless piece of plastic. Then it dawned on me. Our world abounds with Eggy-Weggies, and I cling to them as passionately as Olin did.

Eggy-Weggies can be possessions, prosperity, pleasure, power, or popularity. Perhaps it's owning a Corvette convertible or writing a best-selling novel. But they all have this in common: they're empty and cannot fulfil us. No matter how cool or expensive they are or how much we think we can't live without them.

As strange as it sounds, Eggy-Weggy points us the cross. Prior to Calvary, humanity eked out a meaningless existence (see Ecclesiastes 1:2). But because of the cross and the empty tomb, life explodes with purpose—preparing us for an eternity of joy. Christ's sacrifice transports us from the realm of eternal death into eternal life, from a black-and-white film to one that comes alive in technicolour.

This is why Paul closed the book of Galatians with these words: "As for me, may I never boast about anything except the cross of our Lord

Jesus Christ. Because of that cross, my interest in this world has been crucified, and the world's interest in me has also died" (6:14 NLT). No matter how many Eggy-Weggies I cling to, the cross is all that matters. Laid alongside the cross and the empty tomb, my dearest Eggy-Weggy is a worthless piece of plastic. Nothing else has significance. Only embracing the cross of Jesus will fulfil our deepest longings.

At some point, the memory of Eggy-Weggy faded from Olin's prefrontal cortex. His precious possession is now laid to rest under a thousand tons of rubbish in the Sonoma County landfill. I'm confident my most beloved Eggy-Weggy will suffer the same fate. As Peter states, one day "the elements will be destroyed by fire, and the earth and everything done in it will be laid bare" (2 Peter 3:10).

But what Jesus accomplished on the cross endures forever.

Principle

Compared to the cross and the empty tomb, nothing else matters.

Ponder

- What Eggy-Weggies do you tend to cling to for fulfilment?
- How can you find your fulfilment in the cross of Jesus and the empty tomb?

Pursue: For a deeper dive, study 2 Peter 3.

Lord Jesus, you are all I need. Yet I find myself so easily pulled away by the Eggy-Weggies of this world. Please turn my focus back to you and the salvation Jesus brought me through his death on the cross.

Inky's Escape

An octopus may not have a backbone, but it has a brain—nine brains in fact—as Inky the octopus demonstrated. Inky was a resident at the National Aquarium in New Zealand. One evening, a maintenance worker left the lid to Inky's tank slightly ajar. Seizing the moment, Inky squeezed through the opening and slithered across the floor. He discovered a drain which emptied into the ocean, manoeuvred through it, and returned to the freedom of the open seas. The next morning, technicians discovered the slightly open tank, along with a trail of octopus slime ending at the drain. Inky has not been seen since.[11]

Inky's ingenious escape rivals the likes of any James Bond getaway. On a deeper level, doesn't Inky's daring adventure point to the longing in every creature's heart for freedom? Jesus acknowledged this when he described his mission. "He has sent me to proclaim freedom for the prisoners and recovery of sight for the blind, to set the oppressed free" (Luke 4:18). Jesus died on the cross to free us from the bondage of sin and promised, "If the Son sets you free, you will be free indeed" (John 8:36).

After eternal salvation, perhaps the greatest blessing of the cross is freedom. Freedom from the bondage of sin. Freedom to discover our God-given identity. Freedom to experience the abundant life God intended for each of us (John 10:10).

Whether you're locked up in prison, stuck in a dead-end job, or trapped in a loveless marriage, Jesus offers a new kind of freedom. One that isn't based on external circumstances. One that enables us to rise above the worst situations and soar in the Spirit.

My, how this clashes with the world's view of freedom. (Should we be surprised?) Human culture defines freedom as casting off restraints and doing what we want, when we want, however we want. But look around. How does this philosophy play out in the lives of those who espouse it? Addiction, disease, and heartbreak go hand in hand with this lifestyle. True freedom doesn't come from indulging our flesh, but from submitting to God (Galatians 5:13). By accepting the freedom Jesus offers, we are "free indeed."

The next time you visit an aquarium or zoo, think of Inky and the true freedom that only comes from embracing the cross and following our Saviour.

Principle

Through the cross, Jesus grants us true freedom.

Ponder

- In what area of life have you struggled to feel free?
- How does the promise of Jesus to "set the oppressed free" offer you hope?

Pursue: For a deeper dive, study Galatians 5:1–16.

Lord, thank you for setting me free at the cross.
Help me walk in this freedom each day.

Hope in a Gulag

Aleksandr Solzhenitsyn languished for eight years in a Soviet gulag. After endless days of gruelling conditions and near starvation, he gave up hope. Laying his shovel aside, he sat on a bench, knowing his actions could lead to his death. But he was too weary to care. Any moment, he expected a guard to command him to return to work. When he refused, the guard would beat him to death with his shovel. He had witnessed this fatal punishment many times. Sensing a shadow hovering over him, he braced himself to die.

Instead, he saw an old man standing before him. Weary and weathered, without a word, the man drew a cross in the dust with a stick. Looking into his eyes, Solzhenitsyn understood. The cross represented everything of value in life—hope, joy, purpose, and salvation. Taking a deep breath, Aleksandr nodded at the old man, pushed himself up from the bench, reached for his shovel, and returned to work. Following his release, Solzhenitsyn penned *The Gulag Archipelago*, a source of inspiration and knowledge in the Soviet resistance movement, which affected millions worldwide.[12]

The cross truly is the hope of humankind. Matthew describes the ministry of Jesus to a people living in despair. "A bruised reed he will not break, and a smouldering wick he will not snuff out, till he has brought justice through to victory. In his name the nations will put their hope" (Matthew 12:20–21). Only in the cross of Christ can we find justice, victory, and the hope we long for. This is true no matter who we are, when we live, or where we find ourself in life.

Through the centuries, the story of the cross has lifted the hearts of countless believers worldwide. Whether we live in Russia, Afghanistan, or America, we're surrounded by foes attacking our faith—sometimes in subtle ways, sometimes in not-so-subtle ways. God assured us this would happen (2 Timothy 3:12).

Like Solzhenitsyn, we may grow weary from the oppression we experience. But as our world grows darker, our hope shines brighter. Like the Soviet champion, we know the hope we have in Jesus is all that makes sense in our upside-down world. As we lament the challenging conditions around us, let's focus on the cross, on Jesus, and on the hope we have in him. The cross is our source of strength—whether we're in a cathedral, a home, or a gulag.

Principle

The story of the cross offers hope to every believer.

Ponder

- In what specific situations does the cross offer hope for you?
- How can you point others to the hope of the cross?

Pursue: For a deeper dive, study Matthew 12:15–21.

Lord Jesus, thank you for the life, hope, and victory of the cross, no matter what's happening or where I live. I embrace your cross as my only source of hope and salvation.

Peace Child

Don and Carol Richardson served as missionaries in New Guinea among the Sawi people. The couple laboured to share Christ's love with this tribe, but the Sawis resisted the mercy of God. Their culture didn't value this quality. Missionary historian Ruth A. Tucker wrote, "As [Don] learned the language and lived with the people, he became more aware of the gulf that separated his Christian worldview from the worldview of the Sawi: In their eyes, Judas, not Jesus, was the hero of the Gospels, Jesus was just the dupe to be laughed at." Then Don discovered the concept of the Peace Child, which opened their hearts to the gospel.

Two tribal villages constantly warred, with much bloodshed. Unable to convince them to abandon their violent practices, Don and Carol informed the Sawis they were leaving. This news devastated the tribe, because the Richardsons provided critical medical aid. The Sawi chief took drastic action. He summoned the enemy tribe for a sacred ceremony. As the tribes faced each other, the Sawi chief snatched his infant son from the baby's mother. He placed the child in the arms of the enemy chief. The enemy tribe vanished into the jungle, and the child was never returned.

When the Richardsons asked about the ceremony, the chief explained, "I offered my son as the Peace Child for our tribes. As long as my son lives, there will be peace between us. If he dies, war will resume. Anyone who kills a Peace Child will himself be killed." This practice enabled Don to contextualize the gospel, sharing how God offered his Son as the Peace Child for us. For the first time, the Sawi people grasped the gospel. Hundreds of them gave their lives to Jesus.[13]

We recognise Jesus Christ as God's Peace Child. By accepting him as our Saviour, he restores our peace with God. The apostle Paul described it this way, "Since we have been justified through faith, we have peace with God through our Lord Jesus Christ. . . . While we were God's enemies, we were reconciled to him" (Romans 5:1, 10).

Consider the impact on our lives. Almighty God, our Creator, willingly gave up his Son, so we, his enemies, could live forever in spiritual peace. Jesus is God's one and only Peace Child.

Principle

Jesus is our Peace Child, the only one who can restore our peace with God.

Ponder

- If you were Don Richardson, what would you have thought during this ceremony?
- When have you experienced Jesus as your Peace Child?

Pursue: For a deeper dive, study Romans 5:1–11.

> *Father, thank you for your willingness to sacrifice your only Son as the Peace Child. May I forever live in gratitude for this great sacrifice you made for me.*

Saved by a Rubber Ducky

Ninety-year-old Shirley Madsen of Walnut Creek, California, climbed into the bathtub, anticipating a relaxing soak. However, when the nonagenarian attempted to extricate herself, she was too weak to crawl out. Her phone was out of reach, so calling for help was not an option. Three days later, her concerned daughters arrived on the scene and called an ambulance. Thankfully, their mother was fine. For those three troubling days, she had maintained her body warmth by turning on the hot water tap to replace the cool water. She credits her survival to a rubber duck on the edge of the tub. Shirley remained hydrated by squeezing fresh water into her mouth from the flexible fowl.

In a sense we're all like Shirley—stuck in an impossible situation, powerless to rescue ourselves. We need a Saviour—in the form of a lamb, not a rubber ducky. "The Lamb of God," John the Baptist said, "who takes away the sin of the world!" (John 1:29).

For over a thousand years, the Jews offered lambs as sacrifices to cover their sins. But not really. Hebrews 10:4 states, "It is impossible for the blood of bulls and goats to take away sins." So why would God command the Jews to offer unblemished animals as sacrifices if they couldn't remove sin? To provide a context for Christ's coming and help his people understand their need for a perfect sacrifice. The author of Hebrews refers to these sacrifices as "a shadow of the good things that are coming" (10:1).

Every day in the Jewish temple, priests offered sacrifices at the morning (9:00 a.m.) and evening (3:00 p.m.) times of prayer. Mark tells us Jesus was crucified at 9:00 a.m., precisely when a lamb was sacrificed (Mark 15:25). He died at 3:00 p.m., the moment of the evening sacrifice (15:34–37).[14]

At the exact time when the Jewish priests scurried about offering their "shadow" sacrifices, their companions were crucifying the true Lamb of God, who came to remove our sins. Thank God we have a Saviour who rescued us from our calamity. Rubber duckies are fine if we're stuck in a bathtub and need water. But if we need forgiveness, we'd better look to a lamb—the sinless Lamb of God.

Principle

Jesus is the Lamb of God, our Saviour, who takes away all our sin.

Ponder

- How does understanding Jesus as the Lamb of God help you appreciate your salvation?
- Why do you suppose the Jewish people struggled so much to accept Jesus as God's Lamb?

Pursue: For a deeper dive, study Hebrews 10:1–18.

Sweet Lamb of God, thank you for your sacrifice and the salvation you bring through your death and resurrection.

Rare Coins

Dakoda Garren, a nineteen-year-old man from Washington State, was arrested for stealing a rare coin collection worth over $100,000. Although authorities were certain of his guilt, he was released due to lack of evidence. Then Garren began spending the coins—at face value. He paid for a movie with vintage quarters worth up to $68.00 each. Later, he purchased a pizza using additional rare coins, including a Liberty quarter, valued at over $18,000. His spending spree abruptly ended when he was arrested and jailed.[15]

Besides disobeying God's commandment "Thou shalt not steal," Garren possessed another serious flaw. He failed to value the immense worth of what he possessed.

At times we can all slip into this mindset about our relationship with Jesus. God has given us the most inconceivably valuable treasure anyone ever received: eternal life through the cross. But perhaps we've heard the story of the cross so many times we know the lines by heart, and it becomes ho-hum to us. Familiarity doesn't always breed contempt. It often breeds complacency.

Consider the church in Ephesus. No congregation outside of Jerusalem had more spiritual blessings dumped in their lap. Paul established the church on his third journey and stayed there longer than any other place. He addressed the book of Ephesians to this group, later left Timothy there to serve the church, and apparently sent the epistle of First Timothy while Timothy was ministering to this congregation. According to church history, the apostle John lived among them and cared for Mary, the mother of Jesus, until she died in this city.

With such an abundance of spiritual opportunities, this church must have been overcome with fiery passion for Jesus. But sadly, the apostle John wrote to them, "You have forsaken the love you had at first" (Revelation 2:4).

Although the reasons differ, like Dakoda Garren, we can fail to value our cherished treasure. Like the Ephesians, we can grow complacent towards Jesus, our first love.

The solution? Ask God to restore our passion. Fall on our face each day before him—whether literally or in our hearts. Praise him, thank him, and meditate on our spiritual wealth. Like the Ephesians, we're buried neck-deep in rare spiritual coins. We must treasure the eternal life, given to us freely on the cross, the rare coins of every spiritual blessing we have in Christ (Ephesians 1:3).

Principle

The sacrifice of Jesus is like a valuable rare coin.

Ponder

- What warning signs might alert you to a slow-growing complacency towards Jesus?
- What steps can you take today to remedy this?

Pursue: For a deeper dive, study Revelation 2:1–7.

Dear God, forgive me for my complacency towards the sacrifice of Jesus. Help me never lose the love I had for you when I first accepted your gift of salvation.

Lost

Fresh out of high school, my friend Doug and I joined my dad on a camping trip in the Washington Cascades. After three days, we pitched our tent near a ski lodge. We had arranged for my mum to pick us up there the next day. Doug and I hiked down the hill and called my mum to confirm the arrangements. The sun was setting as we headed back to camp.

During our trip down the mountain, we'd entertained each other with fake Bigfoot sightings. At random intervals, one of us would yell, "There's a Sasquatch!" Such foolishness occupied our juvenile minds for hours. We engaged in deep intellectual debates over the existence of Sasquatches. Now with darkness encroaching, we regretted our earlier conversations. We'd brought only one flashlight because we were certain we'd return to camp before dark. We discovered that no darkness compares with walking in a deep forest on a moonless night. Even the movements of tiny nocturnal animals sound like the noises a Bigfoot might make.

Eventually, our cheap flashlight began to fizzle. Then we realised we'd wandered off the trail. We were hopelessly and helplessly lost in the thick of Bigfoot country. Shivering in our flimsy T-shirts, we were too terrified to bed down for the night. Then our eyes observed a faint glow in the distance, and we pursued the light. Advancing closer, we detected a voice shouting. My dad! We manoeuvred our way to camp, saved by the light and my father's call.

Being lost can leave you feeling hopeless, helpless, and downright horrified. But no other fear compares to the terror of being spiritually lost—separated from God. The apostle Paul declared that without

Jesus, we are "separate[d] from Christ . . . without hope and without God" (Ephesians 2:12). Imagine being cut off from our Creator, unable to pursue the purpose of our existence.

But there's good news. Just as Doug and I followed the light of the campfire, we can follow the light of Jesus (John 1:9). As my father called to us, so our Father's voice calls us to him (Matthew 22:14). We simply need to respond to his call.

The cross is God's answer to our lost condition. Through the cross, God beckons us, calling us to unite with him. As we conclude this section on the cross and move towards the resurrection, remember Jesus has provided a way for us to be rescued from our lostness. Why would we want to stay lost when we can be found?

Principle

The cross is God's answer to our lost condition.

Ponder

- Have you ever been lost? How did it feel?
- Have you responded to God's call to surrender to him?

Pursue: For a deeper dive, study Ephesians 2:1–13.

> *Heavenly Father, thank you for the cross and the salvation you offer through it. Draw me to you by your light and empower me to hear your voice.*

PART FIVE

The Resurrection

If Christ is risen, nothing else matters. If Christ is not risen, nothing else matters.

Jaroslav Pelikan[1]

He has forced open a door that has been locked since the death of the first man. He has met, fought, and beaten the King of Death. Everything is different because He has done so. This is the beginning of the New Creation: a new chapter in cosmic history has opened.

C. S. Lewis[2]

The Resurrection on Trial

World records can be fascinating. For example, consider this post in *The Guinness Book of World Records*: "Most Successful Lawyer: Sir Lionel Luckhoo . . . succeeded in getting his 245th successive murder acquittal."[3] No one has ever come close to duplicating this feat. Luckhoo possessed impeccable analytical skills to dissect flaws in seemingly airtight cases, making him the most successful attorney in recorded history.

As part of his spiritual journey, Luckhoo focused his expertise on the evidence for the resurrection. His conclusion? "I say unequivocally that the evidence for the resurrection of Jesus Christ is so overwhelming that it compels acceptance by proof which leaves absolutely no room for doubt." When the most successful attorney in history applied the test of legal evidence to the case of the resurrection, he concluded without a doubt Jesus rose from the grave. Then, after his search, Luckhoo made another decision—he gave his life to Jesus.[4]

Evidence is crucial for so many decisions. As Lionel Luckhoo discovered, when it comes to choices affecting our eternal destiny, such as the resurrection, the evidence is too overwhelming to ignore.

The people on the day of Pentecost thought so too. Fifty days after Christ's death, Peter stood before a crowd of thousands and declared, "God has raised this Jesus to life, and we are all witnesses of it" (Acts 2:32). This is a bold statement. But consider the evidence. The place where Peter made this declaration was merely a few hundred yards from where Jesus was buried. Suppose Christ's corpse still lay in the tomb. The crowd would have laughed Peter out of town. Someone brash enough could have brought in Jesus' body, plopped it down, and said,

"Here's the body of Jesus. We never want to hear his name again." And the world would never have heard of Jesus of Nazareth. Christianity would have died before it was born.

But that's not what happened. That day, three thousand made the same decision Lionel Luckhoo did. The fact that we've heard of Jesus, the fact that I'm writing this devotion two thousand years later, on the other side of the world, proves that tomb was empty. The evidence is overwhelming, as Lionel Luckhoo discovered. As those on Pentecost discovered. And I'm confident you will also believe the evidence, if you put the resurrection on trial.

Principle

The evidence for the resurrection of Jesus is overwhelming.

Ponder

- How does the story of Sir Lionel Luckhoo affect your view of the resurrection?
- Does someone you know need to hear Lionel Luckhoo's story? Ask God to give you an opportunity to share it.

Pursue: For a deeper dive, study Acts 2:22–41.

Jesus, the evidence for your resurrection is overwhelming.
Help me share this with those around me.

Chocolate Bunnies

The door flew open, and I dashed into the living room—not quite with the thrill of Christmas morning, but excited to see what the Easter Bunny had left. Then I spied my Easter basket, the contents immersed in pink plastic grass: marshmallow chicks, jellybeans, and egg-shaped malt balls. But crowning it all, the queen mother of Easter delights: a chocolate bunny.

My taste buds sprang to life, anticipating a day of culinary decadence, munching for hours on the solid mass of chocolate rabbit. Wiping the drool from my mouth, I attacked the feet first. But one nibble yielded disappointment. The Easter treat wouldn't deliver a day of delectable delights, but merely a few minutes of taste bud titillation. The rabbit was hollow, filled with air, a cruel chocolate façade designed to tempt children—filled with promises, but unable to deliver.

Our lives are crammed full of chocolate bunnies—things promising purpose and pleasure. A new job, a new car, a new relationship. They tantalize us for a few moments, but the happiness they give is short-lived. They fail to deliver when it comes to long-lasting fulfilment.

But not Jesus. While alive, he made some fantastic promises: lives filled with purpose, peace, power, and perpetual life. Then he died. But in contrast to my Easter experience, Jesus delivered on his promises. I awakened on Easter morning expecting something wonderful and was disappointed. His followers awoke that Easter morning in depression and despair—feeling empty and hopeless—but they experienced a surprise more wonderful than they ever imagined.

They trudged to the tomb, expecting nothing—and that's what they found—an empty tomb. But unlike my chocolate bunny, that hollow shell of an empty tomb transformed their lives, filling their hearts with hope and joy. Notice their reactions to the resurrection. "The women hurried away from the tomb, afraid yet filled with joy" (Matthew 28:8). "They still did not believe it because of joy and amazement" (Luke 24:41). "The disciples were overjoyed when they saw the Lord" (John 20:20). Joy, joy, and more joy.

This was quite the opposite of my chocolate bunny experience. If you're searching for purpose and fulfilment in life, don't expect to find it in chocolate bunnies. Ultimately, they'll leave you empty. Instead, look to the empty tomb, which will overwhelm you with joy that will endure for eternity.

Principle

The chocolate bunnies of the world are empty and hollow. The empty tomb gives us purpose and fulfilment.

Ponder

- When have you received a chocolate bunny that left you feeling empty inside?
- How does the risen Christ fulfil your deepest needs?

Pursue: For a deeper dive, study Luke 24:1–12.

Risen Lord, replace the chocolate bunnies of my life with the purpose and power of your resurrection.

Life to Death to Life

My friend Marilyn awoke one morning to learn that she'd been officially dead for several weeks. Her ordeal began when she attempted to renew a prescription. A clerk informed her, "I'm sorry, but you're listed as deceased." Evidently, another woman in the county with Marilyn's name had passed away. Rather than cross-checking her identification, the two women's identities were switched. Even the Social Security Administration failed to confirm my friend's social security number (go figure) to be certain they were dealing with the correct Marilyn. My friend's checking account, annuities, and medications were all frozen.

Seems like restoring her identity would be easy, right? But like being mired in quicksand, Marilyn and her husband, Jim, had stepped into a quagmire of paperwork purgatory. Some days Marilyn spent hours on hold with government agencies, attempting to convince them she was indeed alive. Then the IRS got involved, and let's just say that didn't simplify her situation. After battling layers of bureaucratic blunders for six months, a breakthrough occurred. Marilyn was officially alive again.

In a tiny way, Marilyn's life-to-death-to-life story parallels the resurrection of Jesus. In Revelation 1:18, Jesus told the apostle John, "I was dead, and now look, I am alive for ever and ever!" Obviously, there are huge distinctions between Marilyn's resurrection and that of Jesus. Our Lord's resurrection wasn't some sort of clerical glitch. He *literally* died and *literally* rose from the dead. Never to die again.

Because Jesus rose, we have the assurance of a reward that lies ahead for us. The author of Hebrews writes, "We have this hope as an anchor for the soul, firm and secure. It enters the inner sanctuary behind the curtain, where our forerunner, Jesus, has entered on our behalf" (6:19–20). The word *forerunner* means "one who goes before to prepare the way for others to follow." Like Daniel Boone blazing the trail for settlers, Jesus went before us into heaven, where we will follow.

Except for those alive when Christ returns, there will come a day when *all* of us will die. For real, not because of some careless clerk. My soul will exit my body, and because I am one with Jesus, I will join him in eternal bliss. What an amazing day that will be. In times of trouble, we can cling to this hope. All because Jesus rose from the dead and conquered death forever.

Principle

Jesus was dead but is now alive forever.

Ponder

- During times of trouble, how can you find strength in Christ's resurrection?
- In the midst of exile, how do you suppose Jesus' words, "I was dead, and now look, I am alive for ever and ever!" impacted John's life?

Pursue: For a deeper dive, study Hebrews 6:16–20.

*Lord, free me from my fear of death. Help me
trust you, my resurrected Lord.*

The Transforming Power of the Resurrection

We sat facing each other on opposite sides of the glass. Brian was serving time for drug charges and violence. His bare arms were covered with bizarre, occult-related tattoos. He fidgeted, hoping to get into a recovery program I represented. He said he believed in Jesus and wanted a fresh start. He rattled off a litany of his offences against God—white supremacy, drugs, gang activity, sorcery, and sexual sins. Looking down he asked, "Do you think I'll ever be able to change my life?"

"Only God can change your life," I told him. "As we partner with him, he transforms us."

We all want to change our lives, to rid ourselves of those habits that stick to us like bubble gum on a hot sidewalk. Thank God, through Christ's resurrection power, we can experience transformation. Consider Peter. The night before Jesus died, he cowered before a servant girl and denied he knew Jesus (John 18:16–17). Yet fifty days later, Peter stood before thousands and boldly accused them of killing the Messiah (Acts 2:23–24). What happened? The life-changing power of the resurrection.

Thomas was transformed from doubter to believer (John 20:24–28) and Saul of Tarsus from Christian-killer to world-renowned evangelist (Galatians 1:13–17). Millions through the centuries have experienced similar transformations.

In Ephesians 1:19–20 (NLT), Paul prays, "That you will understand the incredible greatness of God's power for us who believe him. This is the same mighty power that raised Christ from the dead." The same power that reached into Christ's tomb and made his cold, lifeless corpse spring to life is ours for the asking. When Jesus walked out of the grave, he triumphed over death and ended Satan's grip over us.

This is good news for Brian—as well as for godly men and women. The power of our resurrected Lord can transform us. Jesus has already won our battle. We simply need to step into our victory and allow God to change us.

Brian entered the recovery program fully surrendered to Jesus and was baptised. Today he's married with children, owns a business, and leads a ministry serving the homeless. He dreams of opening a ranch for troubled youth. This is the transforming power of the resurrection, made possible because our all-powerful Lord rolled the stone away and walked out of the grave, proving he has the power to transform our lives.

Principle

The resurrection of Jesus has power to transform our lives.

Ponder

- When have you experienced the transforming power of the resurrection?
- Do you know someone who needs this power? What is your prayer for that person?

Pursue: For a deeper dive, study John 20:19–29.

All-powerful Jesus, I stand in need of your resurrection power to transform my life. Please do a work in my heart to make this possible.

"I'll Meet You after the Resurrection"

A story was told of an actor performing the part of Jesus in the Ozarks Passion Play. As he carried his cross, a man from the audience began heckling him. When he persisted, the actor supposedly threw down his cross, walked over, and punched the man. Outraged, the director confronted the performer, warning him against such bizarre behaviour. The next day, the heckler continued his verbal tirade, and again, the actor punched him. The director told him he would be fired if this happened again. The third day, the heckler resumed his ridicule. Restraining himself, the actor snarled, "I'll meet you after the resurrection."[5]

Prior to his death, Jesus told his followers, "After I am raised from the dead, I will go ahead of you to Galilee and meet you there" (Mark 14:28 NLT). His intentions were drastically different from the actor's, but he did indeed meet them "after the resurrection." The Bible reports he appeared to his disciples no fewer than twelve times. On one occasion, more than five hundred people were present when he came to them (1 Corinthians 15:6). These weren't ghost sightings, like those who claim to see Elvis. Jesus physically showed up—walking, talking, even eating with his followers. If each of those five hundred witnesses testified for fifteen minutes in a court of law, the result would be 125 hours of eyewitness testimony.

But how can we know his followers didn't invent this story? First, because many were tortured to death because of their testimonies, yet none recanted their declarations. Many die for a lie, but who dies for a lie, knowing it's a lie?

Also, these witnesses began testifying directly after the resurrection, in the immediate vicinity where the events occurred. Anyone could have easily disproved their testimony if they were lying.

If Jesus' followers fabricated the story, they'd have chosen different witnesses. All four gospel accounts record women as the first witnesses. Don't be offended ladies, but in those days, a woman's testimony was not admissible in a court of law. All these facts point in one direction: Jesus rose from the grave and appeared to his followers.

In a real sense, Jesus still meets us after the resurrection. He brings comfort to us during times of failure, frustration, and fear. Just as he promised his disciples, when we need him most, he whispers to us, "I'll meet you after the resurrection."

Principle

Jesus still meets us today, bringing comfort and encouragement.

Ponder

- When has Jesus met you as the risen Lord?
- How might you need a fresh encounter with Christ?

Pursue: For a deeper dive, study 1 Corinthians 15:1–8.

Risen Lord, I ask that you meet me in my times of need, as you met with your followers after your resurrection.

The Real Jesus

Two elderly sisters from the Russian village of Novonikolsk sobbed as they buried their eighteen-year-old dog, Dik, at a pet cemetery. But shortly after his funeral, Dik awoke and dug his way out of the shallow grave. Someone spotted him on the side of a road and took him to an animal shelter. The two sisters learned of Dik's resurrection and brought him home. Irina Mudrova, head of the shelter stated, "Fortunately, they buried him not deep underground and he managed to get to the surface."[6]

It's happened before. Someone died and was buried, friends grieved for him, then he surprised everyone by rising from the dead. Following his resurrection, Christ first appeared to Mary Magdalene (Mark 16:9). The apostle John tells us, "Mary stood outside the tomb crying" (John 20:11, 14–15). She turned around and saw Jesus standing there, but she did not realise that it was Jesus." She thought he was the gardener.

The text doesn't state why she didn't recognise Jesus. But we do the same today. Like Mary, sometimes all we see is Jesus the Gardener. The world recreates him into the man they want him to be. We also can be blinded to the real Jesus by our false ideas of him.

Perhaps we make him into Jesus the Handyman. If we need something fixed in our lives, just give him a call, and he comes running. Otherwise, we don't require his services. Then there's Jesus in a Box. We praise him on Sunday, then stick him back in his box and tell him to be a "good little Jesus." We don't want him watching late-night TV with us or listening to our conversations with work colleagues. Or how about Jesus the Hypocrite? Someone who claims to follow him misrepresents Jesus by acting like a selfish jerk. Folks walk away believing that's who Jesus is. But none of those are the real Jesus any more than Jesus was the gardener.

On that first Easter morning in the garden, Jesus spoke one word—"Mary"—and in that moment everything changed (John 20:16). Mary realised, *Jesus is alive, and he is so much more than I imagined him to be.* He was all-powerful, knew her and called her by name, and changed her life. Because he was the real Jesus.

He does the same for us. He calls us by name and transforms our lives—changing fear into fortitude, heartbreak into hope, and spiritual ugliness into beauty. He's standing beside us, waiting to open our eyes at the right time in order to see him. He's the real Jesus.

Principle

We can miss the real Jesus when we're surrounded by so many false concepts of Christ.

Ponder

- When have you had a genuine encounter with the real Jesus?
- What false concepts of Jesus might you be most vulnerable to?

Pursue: For a deeper dive, study John 20:1–18.

Dear Jesus, open the eyes of my heart to see you as you really are.

Hope on the Highway

Y ou're watching the Super Bowl, and your team is behind with four seconds left in the game. If they don't score a touchdown, they'll lose. As you bite your nails, the quarterback takes the ball and throws a long pass. You watch it soar into the receiver's arms for a touchdown. Your team has won! But then a referee announces, "The receiver had his foot out of bounds when he made the catch. No touchdown." Your heart sinks lower than your toes. You hold your breath while the refs gather around a video monitor to review the play. Several gruelling minutes later an official announces, "After further review, the touchdown stands." You jump up, throwing your bowl of popcorn into the air in celebration.

On the day of the resurrection, the followers of Jesus experienced a much more intense seesaw of emotions. Two of them were travelling to Emmaus, discussing the day's events. Jesus joined them, "but they were kept from recognising him" (Luke 24:16). They explained their dejected state: "We had hoped that he was the one" (v. 21).

"We had hoped." There's a lot of heartbreak behind these three words. Perhaps the Emmaus Road travellers had been among the throngs who'd celebrated Jesus' triumphal entry into Jerusalem a week prior. Jesus had won the game. But then came the cross, and it seemed like game over.

"We had hoped."

As these disciples walked with Jesus, he "explained to them what was said in all the Scriptures concerning himself" (v. 27). Later they'd comment, "Were not our hearts burning within us while he talked with us?" (v. 32). As Jesus ate with them, "their eyes were opened and they recognised him." Then Jesus disappeared (vv. 30–31). If they'd been holding a bowl of popcorn, they might have thrown it into the air. Immediately, they returned to Jerusalem to share their news with the other disciples. Jesus had restored hope and purpose to their lives.

Jesus loves to show up when we're at our worst—a broken marriage, lost job, financial crisis, or loved one's death. He joins us on our personal Emmaus Road when we've lost hope. Jesus arrives in our moment of defeat and snatches victory out of vanquishment if we'll open ourselves to him. We may not always recognise him, but if we listen to his still small voice, we'll find "our hearts burning within us."

Principle

Jesus meets us on our personal Emmaus Road when we've lost hope.

Ponder

- What does the phrase "our hearts burning within us" mean to you personally?
- When has Jesus joined you on your Emmaus Road?

Pursue: For a deeper dive, study Luke 24:13–35.

Precious Jesus, my heart burns to know you more deeply.
Please reveal yourself and your purpose for me.

Jesus and Sleeping Beauty

The story of Sleeping Beauty fascinates children, but have you ever met an adult who believes it? For some, believing in Christ's resurrection is the intellectual equivalent of espousing the fable of Sleeping Beauty. A Jewish carpenter dies, is buried, and three days later returns to life? Sounds like a fairy tale.

What's the difference? For starters, the story of Sleeping Beauty didn't change the course of history as the story of Jesus has. The enchanted princess's tale isn't the foundation of Western civilization. And millions of people through the ages haven't died defending it. This in itself gives us pause.

Then consider the alternative, which is more unbelievable—that the story of Jesus is a fairy tale. A peasant carpenter from a tiny village convinced twelve unlearned commoners he was God. His followers concocted this bizarre story that he came alive three days after dying. Within fifty days, they persuaded thousands of people the tale was true, in the same city where the events supposedly occurred. These men were tortured because they told this story and eventually died horrible martyrs' deaths for a tale they knew was untrue.

Then the story spread like a brush fire throughout the known world, resulting in explosive growth and radically changed lives. Within a few decades, this dead carpenter had so many followers his movement threatened the Roman Empire, which launched an extensive persecution against the followers, resulting in even greater growth of the movement. Throughout history, millions have given their lives for it. Two thousand years later, two and a half billion people claim to follow this allegedly fraudulent Jewish carpenter. He's the foundation of Western civilization and the most influential figure in history—all because of a lie concocted by twelve uneducated men. Who could believe this?

But there's more. When we follow Jesus, we experience his life-changing power. Consider Saul of Tarsus, a violent persecutor of Christians. He wrote, "Christ Jesus came into the world to save sinners—of whom I am the worst. But for that very reason I was shown mercy so that in me, the worst of sinners, Christ Jesus might display his immense patience as an example for those who would believe in him and receive eternal life" (1 Timothy 1:15–16). The worst of sinners was transformed into one of the greatest evangelists.

Through the centuries, millions of testimonies have been recorded. Addicts freed from bondage, marriages restored, derelict men and women transformed into outstanding citizens. Millions living today can attest to the life-changing power of the resurrection. All because of a story invented by twelve commoners? Right.

Principle

As unbelievable as the story of Jesus' resurrection may sound, the alternative is even more unbelievable.

Ponder

- What part of the resurrection story do you (or someone you know) struggle to believe?
- How does the testimony of changed lives, such as that of Saul of Tarsus, make the resurrection more believable?

Pursue: For a deeper dive, study 1 Timothy 1:12–17.

Lord Jesus, forgive me for the times when my faith grows weak and I doubt the undeniable facts surrounding your resurrection. Please increase my faith.

"Surprise, I'm Alive!"

Imagine sitting in your home when a dead person walks through the doorway. That's what happened to sixty-four-year-old Herzlinde Eissler's family. Herzlinde was admitted to the hospital in Mistelbach, Austria, with stomach pains. Several days later, she discharged herself, wondering why her family failed to visit her during Christmas. What she didn't know was, due to a mix-up, the hospital had told her family she had died. Her son Leopold said, "I could not believe it when she walked in through the front door and the whole family were all sitting around dressed in black and planning the funeral. At least it explains why they could not find the body when we wanted to pay our last respects."[7]

Their shock was only a taste of what the women visiting the grave of Jesus experienced on Easter morning. Mark describes how these women headed to the tomb around sunrise. On the way, they discussed, "Who will roll the stone away from the entrance?" (16:3). When they arrived, they found the stone was rolled away and an angel was sitting in the tomb (vv. 4–5). "'Don't be alarmed,' he said. 'You are looking for Jesus the Nazarene, who was crucified. He has risen! He is not here. See the place where they laid him'" (v. 6). Then, in obedience to the heavenly messenger, the women spread the word.

He has risen! These three words changed the course of human history forever. These simple words prove all Christ's claims are true: He is the Son of God, he came from heaven, and we can experience eternal life through him. Ultimately these claims stand or fall on the resurrection. Christ didn't sort of rise from the dead. Either Jesus is the Son of God with power over death or he's the biggest fraud the world has ever known. The resurrection forever substantiates his claims, leaving no doubt that his followers, like him, will live forever.

We live in confidence and hope, knowing our Saviour lives. Knowing he isn't another madman with a messiah complex. Knowing he, and he alone, conquered death and reigns forever. Knowing no matter how bad things look in life, the story is not over.

There's no way I can possibly express how much this promise means to me. As I wrote this book, my world was turned upside down. My wife went home to be with Jesus after battling Stage 4 ovarian cancer. With great joy, I anticipate being with her for all eternity.

Principle

The resurrection substantiates Christ's claims, proving that we, too, can live forever.

Ponder

- What is the biggest shock you've ever experienced?
- How does the resurrection of Jesus empower you to live a life overflowing with hope?

Pursue: For a deeper dive, study Mark 16:1–8.

Lord, your surprises are always the best. On this day, I especially give thanks for the empty tomb the women encountered on that first Easter morning. Help me live in the hope they found that morning.

Ice Surfing with Jesus

It's amazing how far people can go in order *not* to believe the Bible. Dr. Doron Nof, an expert in oceanography and limnology, along with his team, suggest, that rather than walking on water on the Sea of Galilee, Jesus rode across the lake on a piece of ice. "The unusual local freezing process might have provided an origin to the story that Christ walked on water. Since the springs ice is relatively small, a person standing or walking on it may appear to an observer situated some distance away to be 'walking on water.'"[8]

So, Jesus just *happened* to time his walk on the Sea of Galilee at the precise moment a chunk of ice floated by, which according to Nof, only occurred "several times during the last 12,000 years." Jesus then balanced himself on the ice and allowed the wind and waves to carry him as he ice surfed across the lake. Wouldn't it be easier just to believe Jesus was God's Son and could walk on water?

Nof's opinion sounds like some of the counter-explanations unbelievers offer for the resurrection—even though in biblical accounts no one disputed the empty tomb. The earliest theory was that the apostles stole the body. Jewish officials bribed the guards to say, "His disciples came during the night and stole him away while we were asleep.' . . . So the soldiers took the money and did as they were instructed" (Matthew 28:13, 15).

Let's get this straight. We're expected to believe these professional soldiers fell asleep under penalty of death, the disciples sneaked past them, rolled away the stone, and carried off Christ's body. Then the apostles were martyred for a spreading a story they knew was a lie. Sounds a bit like surfing on ice.

Well, perhaps Jesus' enemies stole his body. Why would they? Because having Christ's body would have disproven the resurrection. They would have paid virtually any amount for his body so they could discredit the disciples' claim. But hide it? Never.

Then there's the Swoon Theory. Jesus didn't die—he merely fainted. In the tomb, he recovered, walked away, and was never heard from again. Let's try that. Beat a man half to death, nail him to a cross, wrap him like a mummy, and place him in a tomb. Then he unwraps himself without using his hands, rolls away a massive stone, and sneaks past the guards.

When we honestly examine these explanations, they're as sensible as Jesus surfing on ice. One alternative remains: Jesus rose from the dead. We can ignore the contortions of logic. It requires more faith *not* to believe in the resurrection than to believe in it.

Principle

It requires more faith *not* to believe in the resurrection of Jesus than to believe in it.

Ponder

- If you were living in the first century and heard the guards' explanation, what would you have thought?
- How does hearing the various counter-explanations for the resurrection increase your faith?

Pursue: For a deeper dive, study Matthew 28:11–15.

Lord Jesus, open the hearts of those around us who choose not to believe in you and your resurrection from the dead.

A Knockout Blow

James Braddock, world heavyweight boxing champion from 1935 to 1937, is known as Cinderella Man. His story stands as perhaps the greatest comeback in boxing history, possibly the greatest in the history of sports. Braddock suffered a heartbreaking defeat in 1929, seriously injuring his right wrist and removing him from contention as a light-heavyweight boxer. Then the stock market crashed, and Braddock lost everything. He went on public assistance and worked on the docks to support his family. As he worked, his left wrist became stronger, giving him an edge over other boxers. He was given an opportunity for one more big fight, which he won, despite overwhelming odds. After several more near-impossible victories, he defeated the champ, Max Baer, in 1935, and was crowned world heavyweight champion.[9]

Braddock has an inspiring story, but his comeback pales in comparison to Jesus'. Satan delivered an apparent death blow to Christ, but our Lord rose from the canvas and dispatched a knockout blow to his opponent. Unlike any human champion, Jesus will never lose his crown. He is the undisputed champion of the universe.

The apostle John describes how Jesus appears to John in his glorified, post-resurrection form (Revelation 1:12–16). His eyes are like laser beams, his voice like Niagara Falls, and his face brighter than the sun. Then Jesus speaks, "I am the First and the Last. I am the Living One; I was dead, and now look, I am alive for ever and ever! And I hold the keys of death and Hades" (vv. 17–18).

What does it mean to "hold the keys of death and Hades"? If someone has the keys to my car, they have complete control over it. They decide where it goes, when it's used, and who drives it. Jesus now has control of Satan's realm. No longer is he little baby Jesus—he's the conqueror of death. If all the volcanoes and bombs on earth exploded simultaneously, the effect would be like a puff of smoke compared to his power.

When Jesus died, he went into Satan's realm, walked up to the devil, delivered a crushing blow, and knocked him out. He snatched the keys from the enemy's hand and freed the captives. Then he walked out of the tomb alive—victorious forever. And we share in his victory. He'll never lose his crown. He made the ultimate comeback. He is our champion forever.

Principle

Jesus made the greatest comeback in history, and he is our champion forever.

Ponder

- How does the story of Jesus' victory over Satan inspire you to trust him more?
- How does knowing that Jesus holds the keys of death and Hades fill you with a deeper level of commitment in your walk with him?

Pursue: For a deeper dive, study Revelation 1:9–20.

My Champion, Jesus, thank you for your victory over our enemy. I trust you, knowing you overcame all obstacles to deliver a knockout punch.

The Shadow of Death

Donald Grey Barnhouse, a pastor in Philadelphia, was returning home with his children from his wife's funeral. He struggled to find words to comfort them in their grief. Then a huge moving van passed them. As the shadow of the truck swept over the car, an inspiration came to Dr. Barnhouse. "Children, would you rather be run over by a truck, or by its shadow?"

They replied, "Well, of course Dad, we'd much rather be run over by the shadow! That can't hurt us at all."

Dr. Barnhouse said, "Did you know that two thousand years ago the truck of death ran over the Lord Jesus in order that only its shadow might run over us?"[10]

A point well taken. Remember as a child making shadow figures with your hands? Camels, birds, and lions. They weren't real. Shadows only temporarily block the light from shining and then vanish. Shadows can surprise us, frighten us, even sadden us, but they can't harm us. Shadows have no substance.

Psalm 23 contains this oft-quoted phrase: "Even though I walk through the [sunless] valley of the shadow of death, I fear no evil, for You are with me" (v. 4 AMP). David uses an interesting choice of words as he speaks of facing death. He understood death was merely a shadow. In the end he would "dwell forever [throughout all my days] in the house . . . of the LORD" (v. 6 AMP).

Because Jesus was run over by the truck of death, he removed the sting of the grave. Death is a shadow, with no power to harm us.

As a minister, I've sat by the beds of dozens of people as they passed into eternity. The difference between those who have faith and those who don't is profound. Those dying without God are often filled with terror. But those who know Jesus possess hope—often even joy. I witnessed this in my wife's death. She said she was "excited" to die and "looking forward" to heaven. She even said she felt sorry for us who remained on earth.

Of course we feel sorrow in someone's passing, but understanding how Jesus conquered death frees us from fear. As Dr. Barnhouse observed, death is a mere shadow.

Principle

Death is a shadow, with no power to harm us.

Ponder

- When have you experienced the shadow of death hovering over someone you love?
- How does knowing death is merely a shadow help you to face the fear of death?

Pursue: For a deeper dive, study Psalm 23.

Victorious Christ, thank you for delivering me from the fear of death. Help me embrace the reality of your resurrection.

Obsessed with Death

Frances Hiller, of Wilmington, Massachusetts, died in the spring of 1900. Several years before passing, she purchased a $30,000 hand-carved coffin and a $20,000 funeral dress—worth a total of nearly one million dollars in today's currency. When guests visited, Frances donned her death attire and climbed in the casket so they might observe the splendour of her future corpse. Eventually, she and her husband, who possessed an identical coffin, were laid to rest in a gaudy mausoleum. Thirty-five years later, the tomb was considered an eyesore and torn down.[11]

My creepy meter spikes reading this story. Picturing this woman in her coffin is the seed for a good horror flick. But setting aside its morbidity, we're compelled to ask a more probing question: Why would someone pour such a fortune into a fancy box and dress that would eventually rot? Misplaced priorities? Obsession with death? A twisted belief that the appearance of our dead body matters?

Scripture is clear that focusing on our earth suit is futile. Our physical bodies simply serve as transitory vehicles for our soul, temporary garments to house the eternal spirit. The apostle Paul described this. "Though outwardly we are wasting away, yet inwardly we are being renewed day by day" (2 Corinthians 4:16). He reminds us, "The corpse that's planted is no beauty, but when it's raised, it's glorious" (1 Corinthians 15:43 MSG). Of course we care for our bodies, but ultimately, they will rot.

When Jesus arose, he received a new glorified body—able to pass through walls, change his appearance, and pop in and out of locations (see Luke 24:30–31). His resurrection paved the way for us to receive new bodies in the afterlife, ones that will match his body. John declares,

"When Christ appears, we shall be like him" (1 John 3:2). A day is coming when those who are dead in Christ will rise from the ground, shed our garments of flesh, and receive new glorified bodies, just as Jesus did.

It's foolish to obsess about anything physical. No matter how much we value this life, no matter how much we cling to the things around us, the material doesn't endure. Even if we possess a coffin and funeral attire valued at a million bucks, it's all going to rot. Praise Jesus for his resurrection and the promise of a new body that will last for eternity.

Principle

It's foolish to focus on our physical bodies because they won't endure.

Ponder

- In what ways might you be focusing too much on the temporal?
- How can you begin placing more emphasis on the eternal?

Pursue: For a deeper dive, study 2 Corinthians 4:16–5:10.

Lord, all around me I see reminders that physical things will not endure. Please use these reminders to focus my heart on what is eternal.

A Living Hope

Strapped for cash, a man in Pittsburgh came up with a brilliant idea. He went into a shop and attempted to pass off a counterfeit bill. Not for a mere hundred dollars—this guy tried to convince a clerk he needed change for a one-million-dollar bill. As you might guess, he encountered some challenges. It probably didn't occur to him that he'd attract some unwanted attention. Or that clerks don't keep a million bucks in their till. Or—and here's the clincher—that there's no such thing as a one-million-dollar bill. When the clerk refused, the man lost his temper, the police were called, and . . . you can figure out the rest.[12]

That crook doesn't exactly qualify as a criminal genius, does he? Lex Luthor has nothing to fear. The man's hopes must have soared as he walked into the shop. But one nay from the clerk plunged his hopes into the Mariana Trench. This is how tenuous false hopes can be.

What a contrast with God's promise in 1 Peter 1:3. He "has given us new birth into a living hope through the resurrection of Jesus Christ from the dead." The counterfeiter had hope—but not the living hope Jesus offers. His hope was deader than a rock in the Sahara. That dude placed his hope in the wrong thing.

We've all been there. We put our hope in a get-rich-quick scheme. Or the promise of a job promotion. Or a new romance. And we fall flat on our face. Why is our hope in Jesus any different? The simple phrase, "the resurrection of Jesus Christ," changes everything. Jesus conquered death, giving us the assurance of living forever. Peter reminds us we have "an inheritance that can never perish, spoil or fade . . . kept in heaven for you" (v. 4). This is where our living hope lies. As Peter's readers faced persecution, they found strength in this promise.

The powers of our world can steal our health, wealth, freedom, family—even our lives. But one thing they can never take from us is our hope. It is literally "out of this world." When we face an impossible struggle and we've lost hope, let's look to our living hope that never perishes, spoils or fades. Placing our hope in anything else only leads to disappointment—like trying to pass off a million-dollar bill.

Principle

We have a living hope because of the resurrection of Jesus.

Ponder

- Other than Jesus, what earthly things or people are you tempted to place your hope in?
- What helps you to focus more on the living hope of Jesus?

Pursue: For a deeper dive, study 1 Peter 1:1–9.

Lord Jesus, I praise you that you rose from the dead and have given me a living hope. Help me look beyond my external circumstances to the hope you offer, which is so much greater than anything I encounter in this life.

It's Not Enough

In a 2015 interview in *Esquire,* a reporter asked Paul McCartney if he felt he still had something to prove. He answered, "Yeah, all the time. And it is a silly feeling. And I do actually sometimes talk to myself and say, 'Wait a minute: look at this little mountain of achievements. There's an awful lot of them. Isn't that enough?' But maybe I could do it a bit better."[13]

Keep this in mind. Paul McCartney is listed in Guinness World Records as "the most successful musician and composer in popular music history."[14] Yet three words characterize his life: *It's never enough.* No matter how much we accomplish, worldly achievement is a bottomless pit of always needing to do more.

Saul of Tarsus found this to be true with religious rule keeping. He rattle off a list of his Pharisaic attainments before meeting Jesus in his letter to the Philippians (3:5–6). Like McCartney, Saul was in the "most successful" category—the best of the best as a heretic hunter. His spiritual pedigree and religious accomplishments opened the door for some of the world's greatest offerings: power, prestige, popularity, human praise. He had it made.

Saul possessed what the world values most. People die chasing after such treasures. They sacrifice health and family in the rat race to get a few more of the kind of goodies Saul had. Nations go to war to obtain these things. But Saul abandoned it all when he encountered Jesus. Saul became Paul.

What on earth would cause someone to walk away from everything people cherish? One simple reason. What Paul found in Jesus was so much greater than anything the world offered that it wasn't worth comparing.

In Philippians 3:7 he declares, "I once thought these things were valuable, but now I consider them worthless because of what Christ has done" (NLT). He has "discarded everything else, counting it all as garbage" (v. 8 NLT). Then he clarifies what he values: "I want to know Christ and experience the mighty power that raised him from the dead. I want to suffer with him, sharing in his death" (v. 10 NLT). This was Paul's purpose. This was his calling—to experience the power of the resurrection.

This alone and nothing else will bring us fulfilment, meaning, and purpose. As Paul the apostle and Paul the Beatle discovered, worldly achievements are never enough. But Paul the apostle discovered the greater truth: when placed alongside the life Jesus offers, everything else pales in comparison. It's like comparing a pile of stinking garbage to a rare jewel (v. 8).

Principle

We can only find purpose in the power of Christ's resurrection.

Ponder

- How does the resurrection of Jesus fulfil your longing for meaning, purpose, and fulfilment?
- In what area of life are you most tempted to seek fulfilment in something or someone other than the resurrected Jesus?

Pursue: For a deeper dive, study Philippians 3:1–14.

Lord Jesus, in the power of your resurrection, I can find all the fulfilment I need. Forgive me for the times when I look to this world for satisfaction. Help me stay focused on you.

He Can Do Anything

I stood with my dad watching a juicer demonstration at a county fair. Squirming with boredom, I noticed a sign at the next booth: Paul Anderson, World's Strongest Man. I weighed my options: meet the strongest man on earth or watch carrots being juiced. I begged my dad. He nodded his consent.

Stepping inside the booth, I gasped. There sat a giant, effortlessly curling a set of dumbbells as big as a VW bug. The massively muscular man smiled and said, "Hey kid, my name's Paul Anderson. What's yours?" He shook my hand, his huge mitt swallowing mine.

My mind went blank. "Uh, uh . . . Barney," I finally managed to spit out.

Pointing to the dumbbells, he asked, "You wanna try?" Bending down, I attempted to lift the weights. Nothing. I tried again. Nada. What was impossible for me was child's play for the world's strongest man.

Right now, think of your biggest challenge—health, marriage, children, a habitual sin, or a work-related issue. That one area of life, no matter how hard you try, that you can't overcome—much like an eight-year-old trying to lift a huge dumbbell. Like Paul Anderson, however, it's effortless for Jesus. He's so much more than the world's strongest man. He's the conqueror of death.

Paul, in Ephesians 3:20, declares that God "is able to [carry out His purpose and] do superabundantly more than all that we dare ask or think [infinitely beyond our greatest prayers, hopes, or dreams], according to His power that is at work within us" (AMP). *That* is a lot of power!

Jesus can handle our worst problem as easily as lifting a toothpick. We don't need to wonder. When he walked out of the tomb, Jesus showed his power over all things. He may not instantly fix our troubles, but the resurrection shows he has the power to do that.

Paul Anderson is a legend. To this day, he holds the record for the greatest weight ever raised off the ground by a human being—6,270 pounds. More than three tons. Before his final attempt at the gold medal lift, he cried out to God, "I must have Your help."[15] Even he bowed the knee to Christ and served him, because he understood Jesus has all power.

I still recall my weakness in Anderson's presence. And I'm reminded of the unlimited strength of the one-and-only Jesus Christ, Son of God, who overcame death through the resurrection. He is more than able to handle any burden I carry.

Principle

Jesus has all power and can do anything.

Ponder

- What's the heaviest burden you're carrying right now?
- How can you surrender it to Jesus and allow him to carry it for you?

Pursue: For a deeper dive, study Ephesians 3:14–21.

Lord Jesus, I praise you for your almighty power. You overcame death and demonstrated your ability to lift the heaviest burden I carry.

PART SIX

The Holy Week

In this section, we'll follow the actions of Jesus day by day during the most important week in the history of mankind. You can follow each day closely beginning the Sunday before Easter and experience what Jesus went through as he prepared for the crucifixion. Join his disciples as they grieved his death and rejoiced in his resurrection.

Somehow we just don't make the same boisterous
fun of Holy Week that we do of Christmas. No
one plans to have a holly, jolly Easter.[1]
Frederica Matthewes-Green

PALM SUNDAY

As we begin Passion Week, we see Jesus riding into Jerusalem encountering throngs of celebrating people who welcomed him as their king. Yet instead of entering on a white horse as a conquering king, he rode on the colt of a donkey as an act of humility, demonstrating his "kingdom is not of this world" (John 18:36).

This event is recorded in all four gospel accounts—Matthew 21:1–11; Mark 11:1–11; Luke 19:28–44; John 12:12–19.

When Jesus Came to Town

On October 15, 1971, music legend Ricky Nelson stepped onto the stage at Madison Square Garden for a rock and roll reunion. The audience cheered at first but then began booing, not because of Nelson's performance but because his appearance didn't match what they wanted. His hair and clothes weren't the same as in the 1950s. Nelson chronicled his woes in his hit song, "Garden Party."[2]

In some ways, this parallels Jesus' experience on Palm Sunday. The road was thronged with crowds jockeying for position to grab a glimpse of the Messiah. The masses were convinced this carpenter was the long-awaited king of prophecy. The throngs spread their cloaks on the road to welcome him. All the promises made to Abraham and David, all the words of the prophets, were teetering on the precipice of fulfilment.

But then Jesus did something strange. "As he approached Jerusalem and saw the city, he wept over it" (Luke 19:41). Not tears of joy, as the text shows. "If you, even you, had only known on this day what would bring you peace," he said (v. 42). Imagine going to a birthday party and the birthday boy stands in the corner wailing. Doesn't quite fit.

Jesus knew within five days the same crowd welcoming him as king would be shouting, "Crucify him!" Like Ricky Nelson, he didn't match what they wanted. The Jews longed for a political king, a military leader who would deliver them from Rome. But God's Son didn't come to temporarily save one nation from another nation's oppressive government. He came to save the world from sin for all time.

God's plan is always much bigger than ours.

So Jesus wept. Because he wasn't the kind of king they wanted.

Because he knew they were rejecting him without knowing it. Because he knew the consequences of their rejection would be catastrophic.

Like the Jews, sometimes we want our own version of Jesus. The Mushy Messiah, who allows us to live however we wish. Or Jack-in-a-Box Jesus, who pops out when we need him but otherwise remains out of sight. Or the Health-and-Wealth Christ, who only preaches happiness.

We don't need a Jesus who makes life easier for a short time. We need Jesus the Saviour who delivers us from sin. The One who knows exactly what we need, not someone who gives us everything we want. The Jesus who wept over his people the day he came to town.

Principle

The Jews rejected Jesus because he wasn't the kind of king they wanted.

Ponder

- In what circumstances do you struggle with wanting God on your own terms?
- How can you avoid making the same mistake the Jews did?

Pursue: For a deeper dive, study Luke 19:28–44.

Lord Jesus, I acknowledge you as Lord of my life. I surrender my will and my life to you. Help me to trust in your perfect plan for my life and for the world.

Get Off Your High Horse

During the Protestant Reformation, Martin Luther and Ulrich Zwingli clashed over church doctrine. One morning as Zwingli sat praying in the Swiss Alps, he noticed two goats standing face-to-face on a narrow mountain path. Unable to back up or move in either direction, eventually one goat lay down and allowed the other to walk over him. Zwingli knew what God was calling him to do. He humbled himself and laid down his right to be right.[3]

Humility is not a quality we normally value. The world teaches us to demand our rights and look out for number one. If anyone had the right to demand his rights, it was Jesus, the Son of God. Thankfully, he didn't buy into that value system.

As he began the final week of his life, Jesus entered Jerusalem in what is often called the Triumphal Entry. During this era, the royal and the wealthy rode horses, preferably white stallions, as a display of opulence and power. But Jesus? The apostle John records, "Jesus found a young donkey and sat on it (John 12:14)." He adds this additional commentary, "At first his disciples did not understand all this" (v. 16).

No kidding. Donkeys were associated with poverty and humility. Certainly not a beast suitable for the King of Kings as he entered God's holy city in triumph. It doesn't quite add up. Would the President of the United States ride to his inauguration in a 1982 Gremlin?

But Christ's kingdom is unlike any other in history. He flips the world's values upside down—or more accurately, right side up—and he calls us to imitate him (see Matthew 5:3–12).

Paul, in Philippians 2:3 says, "Do nothing out of selfish ambition or vain conceit. Rather, in humility value others above yourselves." Like

Zwingli's goat, at times we choose to lay down our pride and humbly yield to others. Not so easy. Serving our spouse? No problem . . . until we don't want to. Showing patience to a disrespectful teen? Effortless . . . until we have a bad day. Controlling our temper? We're Mr./Ms. Calm . . . if nothing upsets us. But if the King of the Universe—the one and only Son of God—could set aside his rights and ride a donkey . . . maybe we should do the same.

Laying down our rights might not change the world, but we might be surprised how much it impacts those around us. Like Jesus, maybe it's time to get off our high horse and ride a donkey.

Principle

God the Father calls us to humble ourselves as Jesus did.

Ponder

- In what relationship do you most often struggle to serve humbly?
- How does the example of Jesus help you choose humility in that challenging situation?

Pursue: For a deeper dive, study John 12:12–19.

*Lord Jesus, thank you for your example of humility.
I'm incapable of humbling myself in my own power.
Please enable me to humble myself as you did.*

MONDAY

Upon entering Jerusalem, Jesus went directly to the temple. After observing the actions of the buyers and sellers hawking their wares in God's holy house, along with the money changers, he headed to Bethany, where he spent the night (see Mark 11:11–12).

He returned the next day and cleansed the temple, driving out the buyers and sellers. This action occurred on two occasions, one at the beginning of his ministry (John 2:13–22) and now at the end (Matthew 21:12–17; Mark 11:15–18; Luke 19:45–48).

In a sense, these events served as bookends of his ministry, marking the purpose of his mission—"set the oppressed free" (Luke 4:18).

Aside from Jesus cursing a fig tree, this is the only recorded event that occurred on Monday of Passion Week.

A Different Side of Jesus (Part 1)

While travelling through Scotland, I stopped at a crosswalk so pedestrians could pass. The driver of a car behind me honked his horn. At the next light, a taxi pulled next to us, and the driver screamed, "Wha' are ya doin'!'" His face was red. He may even have been foaming at the mouth. "Ya don' stop for nobody!" He sounded like an enraged Shrek.

I replied, "Okay, thank you," and stared straight ahead. Instinctively, I discerned it wasn't wise to argue with this angry Scotsman.

Thankfully, Jesus never got angry. Our tender Saviour, welcoming little children. Our Good Shepherd, carrying a wayward lamb on his shoulders. The picture is so serene.

Maybe not quite.

Here's another side of Jesus.

> Jesus entered the temple courts and drove out all who were buying and selling there. He overturned the tables of the money changers and the benches of those selling doves. "It is written," he said to them, "'My house will be called a house of prayer,' but you are making it "a den of robbers.'" (Matthew 21:12–13)

There's no way around it—Jesus was angry. Not exactly the flannel-graph Jesus we were taught about in Sunday school.

Jesus was angry, but he didn't throw an out-of-control fit, like the irate Scotsman. His actions were purposeful. Intentional. Mark 11:11 tells us that upon arriving in Jerusalem on Sunday, Jesus went straight to the temple. He surveyed the merchants' booths and left. He returned on Monday, determined to take a stand against the religious abuse he had witnessed.

In case we forget, Jesus *is* the Son of God. Those hawkers had turned God's house—his *house*—into a place of extortion. Imagine walking in your front door tonight and discovering that a stranger has moved in and converted your home into a brothel and a crack house. Think you'd respond like a gentle shepherd?

Jesus overflowed with righteous indignation at the very thought that the merchants in the house of prayer were driving people away.

Sometimes it's wrong *not* to get angry. Even fuming and furious. Ephesians 4:26 states, "In your anger do not sin." If we love children, for example, we *cannot* ignore child abuse. If we encounter someone abusing a child, we *must* act—even taking radical measures to stop it.

I'm glad Jesus was angry. By chasing out the bad guys, he showed how much he loves and protects his own. We'll explore this further in the next devotion.

Principle

Jesus was filled with righteous indignation when he realised that his "house of prayer," intended to draw truth seekers to him, was driving them away.

Ponder

- How do you react to the angry Jesus portrayed in this text?
- When have you found yourself acting more like the abusive money changers than like Jesus?

Pursue: For a deeper dive, study Matthew 21:12–17.

Lord Jesus, thank you for taking a stand against religious abuse. Help me be bold and courageous in standing against evil.

A Different Side of Jesus (Part 2)

In Milwaukee, a fifty-six-year-old man was arrested for discharging a sawed-off shotgun within the city limits. In a fit of rage, he'd shot his lawn mower because it wouldn't start. I'll bet it didn't start the next time he pulled the cord either.[4]

Proverbs 14:17 states, "A quick-tempered person does foolish things." Like shooting their lawn mower. But responding to evil out of righteous indignation is another matter. It's not only appropriate but necessary at times—as Jesus demonstrated when he overturned the money changers' tables and chased them out of the temple. Mark 11:17 records Jesus' words. "Is it not written: 'My house will be called a house of prayer for all nations'? But you have made it 'a den of robbers.'" God intended that people of all nations should seek him. But temple officials were driving people away.

During Passover, thousands of Jews poured into Jerusalem from around the world. Each family's sacrificial lamb required the priests' approval. Travelling with a live lamb presented untold difficulties. But no worry. Temple officials sold preapproved lambs—at a hugely inflated price.

And the money changers? God's law required a tax of one-half shekel, paid only in Jewish currency (Exodus 30:13). No problem. The temple mafia—I mean officials—gladly exchanged foreign currency for shekels—at an exorbitant rate. Robbery in the name of religion.[5]

Travellers journeyed hundreds of miles at great expense to encounter God. And what did they find? Temple officials, like a bunch of loan sharks, demanding payment. God's righteous anger is kindled when someone takes advantage of another in his name. Anyone who comes between God and his children faces harsh consequences. Jesus said, "If anyone causes one of these little ones—those who believe in me—to stumble, it would be better for them if a large millstone were hung around their neck and they were thrown into the sea" (Mark 9:42).

In the temple, Jesus stepped in. He flipped the tables of the money changers and scattered the sheep. He was done with their games, and he made it clear where God stood. This action sealed his fate. A prophet who cut into their profit could no longer be tolerated.

Jesus' actions demonstrate he doesn't want anything to come between us and the Father. I'm thankful for his actions, thankful he was angry, thankful for this other side of Jesus.

Principle

Jesus is willing to step in and protect us from those who prevent us from coming to God.

Ponder

- Describe how you feel, knowing Jesus is willing to go to any extent to protect you spiritually.
- In what ways can you have less religiosity and more spirituality in your interactions with the seekers God brings into your life?

Pursue: For a deeper dive, study Mark 11:15–19.

Lord Jesus, thank you for this different side of you. Thank you for being willing to step in and protect me from those who prevent me from coming to you—especially when they do so in your name.

TUESDAY

Tuesday was a tumultuous day for Jesus, filled with activity. Upon entering the temple, he was confronted by the religious leaders, who questioned his authority to teach. After a series of parables, Jesus denounced their hypocrisy. He then observed people placing their money into the temple treasury and praised a poor widow.

Following this, Jesus headed up the Mount of Olives, where he delivered what is known as the Olivet Discourse on the destruction of Jerusalem and on the end times.

These events are recorded in Matthew 21:23–25, 46; Mark 11:27–13:37; Luke 20:1–21:38; and John 12:20–50.

Fake Fronts

On June 17, 2013, world leaders met for the G8 summit in Ennis Killen, Ireland. The town went to great lengths to spruce up its appearance in preparation for the event. This included setting up fake shop fronts to give the illusion of a thriving business climate. In reality, many shops had closed due to a severe economic downturn. Rather than showcasing the truth, the image-conscious town leaders opted for pretension. A fake front.[6]

The religious leaders of Jesus' time perfected the art of pretence. Like someone hiding behind a cardboard Elvis, the self-righteous Pharisees put on a fake front, pretending they had achieved perfection. All those they considered sinners needed to imitate them. It was religious arrogance of the worst sort. At least Jesus thought so.

After contending with the Pharisees for three years, Jesus unloaded on them. He called them a "brood of vipers" (Matthew 23:33). He said that they were like shiny cups on the outside but filthy on the inside (v. 25). Then he compared the pompous Pharisees with whitewashed tombs with lovely exteriors but rotten below the surface (v. 27).

Seven times he called them "hypocrites," which literally means "actors." They were pretenders, playing games with people's souls rather than serving as spiritual guides for the masses.

Why was Jesus so critical of them? Because he loved those men. For three years, they'd witnessed his miracles, heard his teachings, and observed his character. Yet they criticized and condemned him. Jesus continually reached out to them, but their hard hearts refused to accept him. Two nights later these men would arrest him, so Jesus attempted, one last time, to shake them into repentance with the harshest recorded words he ever uttered. But they refused to open the door a tiny crack to God's Messiah.

Amazing. Each day these religious leaders entered the temple and prayed for God to send the Messiah. Meanwhile, the Messiah was, at that very moment, in the temple courtyard teaching. Then, after killing him, they returned to praying for God to send him. They were too blind to see they'd murdered the answer to their prayers.

Let's learn from the Pharisees' error and forever have "eyes to see and ears to hear" what Jesus is saying to us. May God guard us against spiritual arrogance.

As far as we know, Jesus never returned to the temple. He closed his sermon by saying God's house was empty (v. 38). With Jesus' departure, it was official—God had left the building.

Principle

May we have eyes to see and ears to hear what Jesus is saying and avoid spiritual arrogance.

Ponder

- What false fronts do you tend to hide behind?
- When have you found yourself guilty of spiritual arrogance?

Pursue: For a deeper dive, study Matthew 23.

Lord Jesus, your words to the Pharisees are sobering. Guard me against spiritual arrogance and my tendency to hide behind false fronts.

Radical Generosity

As long as I live, I'll never forget the widow I encountered in India. After teaching at a small village in India, our team was praying for the townsfolk. Limping up to me, with a smile as bright as sunshine, she pressed a small object into my hand. I looked down and discovered it was a half-rupee, worth about a penny. I stared in disbelief. Before I could thank her, she hobbled away. This poor widow, even in deep poverty, was so blessed by Jesus that she shared her wealth with a rich American who didn't need her money.

I turned aside and wept as my mind recalled another widow. Following his final confrontation with the Pharisees, "Jesus sat down opposite the place where the offerings were put" (Mark 12:41). He observed wealthy men depositing large amounts in the temple treasury. Then a poor widow dropped in two coins worth less than a penny. Jesus said, "This poor widow has put more into the treasury than all the others. They all gave out of their wealth; but she, out of her poverty, put in everything—all she had to live on" (vv. 43–44). The disciples must have shaken their heads in confusion, clueless about his meaning.

Two things stand out. First, Jesus' mental wherewithal to continue a conversation following his heartrending confrontation with the Pharisees. Second, the huge gulf that exists between the values of his kingdom and those of our world. A widow's mite possesses greater value in God's eyes than the wealth of the well-heeled aristocrats? Absurd. As the time of his death neared, Jesus wanted his followers to understand what mattered most to him.

Generosity is not connected to how much we possess. Neither is greed. On the same trip to India, we presented ballpoint pens to everyone we encountered. At one meeting, I observed a pastor's wife snatch a free pen from the hand of a disabled orphan girl. Greed can ooze from the pores of anyone, at any time, in any culture.

In prosperity or poverty, a penny or a pen, generosity and greed are heart conditions unrelated to the size of our financial portfolio. I learned this profound lesson from two women in India. I've kept my personal widow's mite to this day. That half-rupee is a reminder of how rich one can be living out the kingdom value of radical generosity.

Principle

Generosity and greed are unrelated to the monetary wealth we possess.

Ponder

- In what ways do you need to practice radical generosity?
- How can you open yourself up for Jesus to transform you from a mindset of greed to one of generosity?

Pursue: For a deeper dive, study Mark 12:41–44.

Lord Jesus, thank you for pointing out the radical values of your kingdom that I struggle with. Please root out any speck of greed in my heart and replace it with a generous spirit.

WEDNESDAY

No events are recorded on Wednesday of Passion Week. Most likely Jesus rested in the home of Martha, Mary, and Lazarus, spending time with his dear friends, before facing the final night before his crucifixion.

This section focuses on two events that apparently took place late on Tuesday, one day prior. They are connected with Mary, Martha, and Lazarus.

These events are recorded in Matthew 26:1–16, Mark 14:1–11, Luke 22:1–6, and John 12:1–8.

Flowers for Jesus

My wife loved receiving flowers from me. Occasionally, I'd stop and pick some up as a gift. Imagine if I handed her a beautiful bouquet and said robotically, "Linda, as your husband, I recognise that you require flowers from me, so I herewith bestow on you said flowers. On the fifteenth of each month, I will deliver to you a fresh bouquet, thus fulfilling my duty to you as your husband." Want to guess how she would have reacted? Probably by throwing them in my face.

But suppose, as I handed her the flowers, I smiled, looked into her eyes, and said, "Linda, words can't express how much I love you. I passed a flower stand and felt compelled to stop and purchase this beautiful bouquet. Just a token of my deep love for you." Now, how would she react? She would smother me with kisses.

What's the difference? Either way, she received flowers. One was a contractual agreement, based on duty. The other was an overflowing expression of love. Flowers aren't really what Linda wanted. She wanted an affirmation of my love.

Perhaps this example helps us understand how Mary of Bethany felt. Jesus attended a banquet in the hometown of Martha, Mary, and Lazarus (John 12:1–5). "Mary took about a pint of pure nard, an expensive perfume; she poured it on Jesus' feet and wiped his feet with her hair. . . . It was worth a year's wages" (John 12:3, 5). A tidy sum.

What would prompt Mary to bestow such an extravagant gift on Jesus? The same reason I gave Linda flowers—it was a heartfelt expression of love. Earlier, Jesus had raised Mary's brother from the dead, instantly transforming her world. Overwhelmed with love, she grabbed an alabaster jar of perfume. Prior to this, it was perhaps her most valuable possession. But now, compared to Jesus, it meant nothing. With a heart abounding with thankfulness, she couldn't *not* do this.

Like Mary, when we realise how much Jesus has done for us, our hearts are stirred to give him "flowers"—not as a have-to, out of religious duty or fear. We're motivated by pure love for the One who freed us. When we consider the magnitude of Christ's grace and mercy, our hearts are overwhelmed. We embrace the forgiveness, freedom, and future Jesus offers and joyfully respond by giving "flowers" to Jesus.

Principle

Understanding what Jesus has done for us stirs our hearts to pour out extravagant love on him.

Ponder

- When has your heart been stirred to demonstrate extravagant love like Mary?
- What perfume can you pour out on his feet?

Pursue: For a deeper dive, study John 12:1–8.

Precious Jesus, words alone are not enough to express my gratitude for all you've done for me. Reveal to me the perfume I value so I can pour it out on you, like Mary did.

The Bitterness of Betrayal

While duck hunting on the north end of the Great Salt Lake, a forty-six-year-old man and his dog were drifting in a small boat. Stepping into the marsh, he left his shotgun resting across the boat's bow. Apparently, the excited dog stepped on the gun, causing it to discharge. His master was shot in the buttocks with twenty-seven pellets of bird shot. Local police are calling the incident an accident, but the dog isn't talking.[7]

Did the owner feel betrayed when he realised what his dog had done? We may chuckle at the irony of man's best friend shooting his owner, but real-life betrayal is no laughing matter—just as Jesus must have sensed the evening after Mary of Bethany anointed him. While the perfume's aroma wafted through the room, the stench of betrayal filled Judas' heart. Immediately after the meal, "Judas Iscariot, one of the Twelve, went to the chief priests to betray Jesus to them" (Mark 14:10).

Scripture doesn't say why the disciple did such a diabolical deed. But consider this: Judas believed Jesus was the Messiah. He'd witnessed him walk on water, calm storms, and raise the dead. Judas was poised for a prominent position in Christ's new administration. But Jesus was moving slowly. Perhaps Judas decided to force his hand. He would betray his Lord; Jesus would establish his kingdom; then Judas would slip back into Jesus' good grace and, in the process, pocket a bit of coinage.

Scripture points to this. Matthew writes, "When Judas, who had betrayed him, saw that Jesus was condemned, he was seized with remorse and returned the thirty pieces of silver" (27:3). Judas wasn't sorrowful until Jesus was condemned because he didn't believe Jesus would die. But regardless of his motive, only a man with a heart as hard as a hammer would sell out his best friend.

Betrayal wasn't necessary for Jesus to save us. So why did he deliberately choose as his disciple someone he *knew* would betray him? (See John 6:70–71.) Because we all experience the bitterness of betrayal. A spouse is unfaithful. A friend gossips. A child rejects our values. When we cry out to God during this gut-wrenching anguish, we have someone in heaven who understands. A friend turned away from him, turned his back on him, and turned him over to his enemies. No pain is more potent. No hurt as horrible. Jesus knows how you feel because God himself experienced the bitterness of betrayal.

Principle

Jesus understands how we feel when we are betrayed because he also experienced betrayal.

Ponder

- When have you experienced the bitterness of betrayal?
- How can looking to Jesus help you move past it?

Pursue: For a deeper dive, study Matthew 27:1–10.

Jesus, during times of betrayal, help me look to you
for comfort and find the strength I need.

MAUNDY THURSDAY

This day is known as Maundy Thursday, *maundy* meaning "commandment," referencing Jesus' commands to his disciples to wash one another's feet and to "love one another" (John 13:14–17, 34–35).

On this day, we observe the final night of Christ's life, an evening packed with activities. These include the Passover meal; the Lord's Supper; his final discourse with his disciples; his agony in Gethsemane; his betrayal, arrest, and trial before the Jewish council; and Peter's denial.

Matthew 26:17–75, Mark 14:12–72, Luke 22:7–65, and John 13:1–18:27 record these events.

Bigger Than Us

Washington, DC, abounds with dazzling monuments depicting great leaders and events. But none compares to a memorial created by Jesus the night before he died. Not a memorial of bronze or marble destined to deteriorate but one composed of the simplest elements: bread and wine. Commonly called Communion or the Lord's Supper, this memorial has been observed by someone, somewhere every day for two thousand years, even if only in their heart.

The ceremony began in an upper room. Jesus gathered with his disciples to celebrate Passover. During the meal, he dropped a spiritual grenade: "One of you will betray me" (Mark 14:18). In the context of this bitter announcement, communion was born.

There's something significant in Christ's timing. These are his most beloved friends. But as he scanned the room and looked into their eyes, the results were heartbreaking. He saw their leader, Peter, and knew Peter would deny him three times before the night ended. He saw their treasurer, Judas, and knew Judas had bargained with his enemies to betray him. He saw the others, and knew they'd all run away like scared children when he needed them most.

John writes, "Jesus was troubled in spirit" (John 13:21). The Greek word translated "troubled" means "acute emotional distress." Yet Jesus looked past his heartbreak to a deeper purpose. He focused on the Father's eternal plan he was preparing to fulfil. He took bread and wine and instituted communion (Mark 14:22–25). He set aside his personal pain to share with his disciples the reason he had entered our world.

Understanding the reason for communion transcends everything we experience in life. It's bigger than us—just as it was for Jesus. Bigger than marriage, childbirth, or a new house. Bigger than our trouble with finances, marriage, work, or kids. My problems appear minuscule when laid alongside God's eternal purpose. God became man and died for me so I could live with him forever. Nothing is bigger than this.

In a few hours, his disciples would witness their master being arrested, beaten, condemned, and crucified. They were on the precipice of facing the forces of darkness in unimaginable, nightmarish scenarios.

But Jesus could look past his suffering and see our salvation. And so can we. When we celebrate communion, we can set aside the good, the bad, and the ugly in our lives, knowing the meaning of the bread and wine truly is bigger than us.

Principle

Celebrating communion is bigger than us.

Ponder

- Under what circumstances do you find it difficult to take communion?
- What practices or habits might make communion more meaningful for you?

Pursue: For a deeper dive, study Mark 14:12–26.

Lord Jesus, I'm in awe of how you set aside your personal pain that night and focused on helping your disciples remember God's eternal purpose. Help me do this, not only when I partake of communion, but every day.

Jesus Knows Injustice

The young woman sat across from me, head down, unable to look me in the eye. Anger and shame practically oozed through her pores. My heart broke for her as she recounted horrific incidents of childhood abuse. On one occasion, her mother's boyfriend sexually molested her. When the girl informed her mum, she beat her daughter, accusing her of lying. Such injustice drove the young woman to seek relief in drugs and a series of lovers, most of whom abused her. Fortunately, she found healing in Jesus.

Jesus also experienced injustice. After being dragged away from the garden, he was hauled from one kangaroo court to another. His verdict had been predetermined. Days earlier, the Jewish high council had met and decided the outcome of his trial: he must die (Matthew 26:3). His night in court was a mere formality, a façade of justice, a mockery of truth.

During that night, Jesus endured six trials. A private examination before Annas (John 18:13); then another with Caiaphas (John 18:24). After the Sanhedrin officially met at sunrise (Matthew 27:1), the Jewish leaders brought Jesus to Pilate, the Roman governor (Matthew 27:2), who promptly sent him to King Herod (Luke 23:7), who returned him to Pilate for the official verdict (Luke 23:11).

This process violated principles of Jewish and Roman law on several levels: they examined him privately (twice), forced Jesus to testify against himself, and struck him when he remained silent. All this injustice was inflicted on the only perfect man who ever lived.

Perhaps the most frustrating part for Jewish leaders was how the witnesses contradicted one another. Mark states, "The chief priests and the whole Sanhedrin were looking for evidence against Jesus so that they could put him to death, but they did not find any. Many testified falsely against him, but their statements did not agree" (14:55–56). The false witnesses couldn't get their lies straight. At that point, the law required that Jesus be released.

Have you ever experienced some form of injustice? We've all found ourselves accused of something we didn't do. We attempt to vindicate ourselves, but no one believes us. During those times, there is someone who understands and listens to our cries: our Saviour Jesus. He suffered every form of injustice. Jesus is our Advocate—our defence attorney (1 John 2:1). He understands our situation better than anyone else, because Jesus knows injustice.

Principle

Jesus understands how we feel when we suffer injustice because he experienced every form of injustice.

Ponder

- At what times or in what situations have you been treated unjustly?
- How does knowing that Jesus experienced severe injustice help you deal with the injustice you've suffered?

Pursue: For a deeper dive, study Mark 14:53–65.

> *Lord Jesus, I take comfort in knowing that you understand my plight. When I experience injustice, remind me of what you went through on that horrible night before you died.*

GOOD FRIDAY

This day is known as Good Friday because on this day our Saviour died, paying the cost of all our sins. Not only is it "good," it's the greatest, most important day in human history because we were delivered from the eternal bondage of Satan.

The events of this day are recorded in Matthew 27:1–56, Mark 15:1–41, Luke 22:66–23:49, and John 18:28–19:37.

A Twisted Kiss

You can't blame the doctor. He did everything possible, yet the damage was irreversible. Dr. Richard Selzer removed a tumour from a young woman's cheek. In the process, he had to sever a tiny nerve controlling the movement of her mouth. As a result, the side of her lip was distorted, sagging noticeably.

Post-op, Dr. Selzer entered her room. With her young husband at her side, she sat in bed, staring in a mirror. Through tears, she asked, "Will my mouth always be like this?"

"Yes, it will," Selzer answered. "It is because the nerve was cut."

She nodded in silence. But her husband smiled, as if they were the only two people on earth. "I like it. It's kind of cute."

Then Seltzer observed, "Unmindful, he bends to kiss her crooked mouth and I am so close I can see how he twists his own lips to accommodate hers, to show her that their kiss still works."[8]

This is much more than a love story between two people. It's the story of Jesus and his bride—his church (Ephesians 5:25–32). Two thousand years ago, God twisted himself to accommodate our needs by climbing into the skin of a human being and entering our world. Then on a hill outside Jerusalem, God again distorted himself in one preeminent act of unconditional love by allowing his body to be twisted into the form of a cross. Taking upon himself all our sins, 2 Corinthians 5:21 states, "God made him who had no sin to be sin for us." The ultimate deformity—a sinless God assuming the guilt of every sin ever committed by every human.

In our opening story, rather than abandoning his bride to her fate, the woman's husband willingly chose to twist his own body to accommodate her needs. Jesus did this for us. Isaiah wrote, "It was our sins that did that to him, that ripped and tore and crushed him—*our sins*! He took the punishment, and that made us whole. Through his bruises we get healed" (Isaiah 53:5 MSG).

Do you suppose the young bride felt loved? Undoubtedly. Likewise, the cross forever proves God's love for us. When we doubt, remember this story. Remember the young husband twisting his lips to kiss his wife. And remember our Saviour being contorted in anguish, hanging between heaven and earth, bestowing on us the ultimate twisted kiss.

Principle

Jesus twisted himself into the form of a cross, in the ultimate act of unconditional love, to save us from our sins.

Ponder

- When do you find yourself doubting God's love?
- How does focusing on the cross deepen your understanding of God's perfect love?

Pursue: For a deeper dive, study Isaiah 53:4–6.

*Lord Jesus, when Satan fills me with doubt, centre my
mind on the love you displayed for me on the cross.*

The Shock of the Cross

A fourth-grade boy was flunking math, and nothing his parents did motivated him. As a last resort, they enrolled him in a parochial school. Coming home after his first day, he ran straight to his room and began working on math. Emerging for a quick supper, he hurriedly returned to complete his homework. Day after day, he repeated this ritual, until he brought home his report card. Amazed to see an A in math, his parents asked, "What turned your grade around? Was it your teacher? The curriculum? The nuns?"

"No. It's because they're really serious about math at this school! When I first walked into the lobby and saw a guy nailed to a plus sign on the wall, I knew they meant business!"[9]

Hanging on a real cross was no joke—and that's the point of this story. God intended for the cross to shock us. Scholars agree that crucifixion was the most shameful and degrading form of death known to ancient man:

Crucifixion? So abominable a deed that no word can adequately describe it. (Cicero)

The most pitiable of deaths. (Josephus)

A matter of subjecting the victim to the utmost indignity. (Martin Hengel)[10]

Crucifixion was so abhorrent in ancient times that no one in polite society mentioned the word. We've sanitized the cross by ignoring its gruesome and degrading nature to make it palatable to our twenty-first-century sensibilities.

But God deliberately selected this painful and shameful method for his Son's death. The writer of Hebrews described how, "he endured the cross, scorning its shame" (12:2). Paul states in 1 Corinthians 1:18, "The message of the cross is foolishness to those who are perishing, but to us who are being saved it is the power of God." Then he adds, "But we preach Christ crucified; a stumbling block to the Jews and foolishness to Gentiles" (v. 23).

Why is the crucifixion "foolishness"? The idea that God would die—especially in such a despicable manner—is too shocking for many to accept. Sheer foolishness. Perhaps this is the point. Jesus was willing not only to endure the agony of the cross, but also to embrace its degradation to demonstrate the depths of his love. Perhaps we should abandon our sanitized view of the cross. Perhaps, like the boy in our story, we need to be shocked into action by it.

Principle

God the Father chose a way for his Son to die that was shocking and shameful.

Ponder

- How do you feel, knowing that Jesus endured such a shameful death?
- What actions can you take to demonstrate your gratitude to Jesus for dying in such a horrible manner?

Pursue: For a deeper dive, study 1 Corinthians 1:18–31.

Lord Jesus, I am forever grateful that you endured the shame of the cross. Help me find ways to express my gratitude every day.

HOLY SATURDAY

Little is recorded about the events of Saturday. On Friday evening, Joseph of Arimathea had asked for Jesus' body. He and Nicodemus wrapped his corpse in linen, coated it in seventy-five pounds of spices, placed it in Joseph's personal tomb, and rolled a stone over the entrance. The women who followed Jesus observed this. How their hearts must have sunk in despair. Now, Jesus' body lay in the tomb. None of them knew the greatest surprise in history awaited them.

Early on Saturday, the Jewish leaders asked Pilate to place guards at Jesus' tomb to ensure no one would steal his body.

These events are described in Matthew 27:57–66, Mark 15:42–47, Luke 23:50–56, and John 19:38–42.

The Saddest of Saturdays

Typically known as Holy Saturday, this day is wedged between Good Friday and Easter Sunday. The Bible records only one sentence describing the disciples' activities that day. "They rested on the Sabbath in obedience to the commandment" (Luke 23:56). John's gospel sheds a little light on their overall frame of mind. It states on the next day, "The disciples were together, with the doors locked for fear of the Jewish leaders" (John 20:19). I suspect the same was true on Saturday. It was perhaps the saddest day in history. The Son of God was dead.

There the disciples sat, hunkered down, huddled together, fearful for their lives. Their grief must have been palpable. Not only were they mourning the loss of their beloved friend and rabbi but also the death of their dreams, the passing of their purpose, the extinction of their hope.

Imagine the scene with me. Staring blankly into space with tears filling their eyes—someone might have occasionally broken the silence. "I just can't believe it. We were all so sure he was the One." Then they slipped back into stillness, grief overtaking them like a dark fog.

Then another might have spoken, "Why did he let them kill him? He didn't even resist. He had the power. We all saw him work miracles." Then more silence. The hearts of the disciples and women must have weighed on them so heavily, they could scarcely breathe. The hours dragged by in an endless parade of grief—and waiting. But waiting for what?

We've all known grief—or at least we will. Times when we have no words to utter—no hopeful thoughts we can muster. We try to pray, but we can't form our thoughts into words.

God could have instantly raised Jesus to life as his body was lifted from the cross—thus combining Good Friday and Easter into one gigantic celebration. Instead, his plan required the disciples to endure the agonizing ordeal of Saturday.

Why? Perhaps so they could learn to trust God. God loves to come through in ways we could never have imagined during our dreadful Saturdays. Paul said in 2 Corinthians 5:7, "We live by faith, not by sight." We trust God when our Saturdays seem darkest. If we understood God's ways, we wouldn't be walking by faith.

I understand the disciples' feelings as I grieve the loss of my wife. But like those first-century followers, God has some amazing surprises in store for his modern-day disciples amid our sorrow. Our grief is for a moment, but our joy together is eternal. We need to remember this truth—even on our saddest of Saturdays.

Principle

We can trust God even on our saddest of Saturdays.

Ponder

- When have you experienced grief similar to these original disciples?
- How does picturing the grief of the early disciples help you in your moments of grieving?

Pursue: For a deeper dive, study 2 Corinthians 5:1–10.

Almighty God, you see everything and know everything. Help me understand that in my grief you haven't abandoned me, just as you didn't forsake your first-century followers. Help me trust your perfect plan.

The Beauty of Burial

Before we saw them, we heard them—their songs of praise in Amharic—lifted to heaven like a symphony. Then a flood of humanity poured over the hills, down to where we waited in a muddy Ethiopian River. These believers had walked for miles to be baptised. By the time our team finished, four hundred had confessed Jesus as Lord, been plunged into a watery grave, and raised into a new life. A perfect picture of the death, burial, and resurrection of Jesus.

On this Easter Eve, we focus on the burial of Jesus. Sometimes as we hurry towards the empty tomb, we pass over his burial. It doesn't possess the profound significance of his death or the triumph of the resurrection. But before we rush into Sunday morning, let's pause and consider the beauty of his burial.

Normally, we don't think of burial as a thing of beauty. As a body is lowered into the ground, some may see it as painful, creepy, even macabre. But beautiful? When it comes to the Easter story, Christ's burial is a beautiful prelude to his resurrection—and a critical piece in the story.

Seven hundred years before Jesus came, Isaiah prophesied of his burial. "He was assigned a grave with the wicked, and with the rich in his death" (Isaiah 53:9).

Even more, his burial is a crucial part of the gospel. In 1 Corinthians 15:1, 3–4, Paul identifies the gospel as the death, burial, and resurrection of Jesus. He writes, "I want to remind you of the gospel. . . . that Christ died for our sins according to the Scriptures, that he was buried, that he was raised on the third day." Obviously, without the tomb, there would be no empty tomb.

Jesus' burial is so significant that God commands us to reenact his death, burial, and resurrection through baptism. Paul wrote in Romans 6:4, "We were therefore buried with him through baptism into death." More than a symbol, in baptism we are supernaturally united with Jesus (v. 5). Baptism is our response to his death, burial, and resurrection.

Pause and meditate on his burial. Picture Christ's cold, lifeless corpse, lying in that dark tomb. In his burial, Jesus connects with our seasons of darkness, when it feels as if we'll be buried forever—helpless and hopeless. During those times, we must remember, it's all temporary. In a few hours, everything changed.

Principle

The burial of Jesus is a critical piece in the Easter story.

Ponder

- When have you felt hopelessly buried?
- How does the burial of Jesus offer you hope amid spiritual darkness?

Pursue: For a deeper dive, study Romans 6:1–7.

Lord, thank you for your amazing plan, which includes Christ's burial as well as his resurrection. Help me find hope during my dark days.

EASTER SUNDAY

Words fail when we attempt to describe this day—the most triumphant, victorious day of liberation in the history of mankind. On this day, Jesus rose from the grave, demonstrating his power over death forever and sealing our salvation. Had Jesus not risen, his life would have been nothing but the sad story of a Jewish peasant with a Messiah complex who was tragically martyred. None of us would have heard of Jesus of Nazareth. But his resurrection changed everything. Because he arose, death is not the end of life, but only its beginning. Now we have the hope of everlasting life with our Lord in heaven.

Matthew 28, Mark 16, Luke 24, and John 20–21 record the resurrection and appearances of Jesus.

Didn't See *That* Coming!

The first rays of dawn were peeking over the hills surrounding the city. Like reluctant children on the first day of school, four women trudged towards the tomb of Jesus. They held aloes and myrrh to anoint the burial wrappings surrounding his body. Their sandals felt lead filled with each step—a reflection of the burden on their hearts. Jesus was dead. Their messianic hope in Jesus had been crushed on a Roman cross.

Lumbering along, they discussed how they could move the huge stone blocking the entrance. They couldn't pry it open, and it would be impossible to roll. Besides, soldiers were guarding the entrance. What could four women do? Why did it matter? Jesus was dead.

The women turned the corner leading into Joseph's private garden, and the tomb came into view. They froze in their tracks. The tomb was open. Questions raced through their minds as they stood stunned. What happened? Where's the stone? Who could have done this? Mary Magdalene ran to get Peter.

The other three crept towards the opening. They peeked inside and were shocked to see Jesus' burial wrapping lying fully intact—but completely empty! It was still covered with the seventy-five pounds of spices Joseph of Arimathea and Nicodemus had applied (John 19:39–40). The stiff wrappings maintained the shape and form of a human body—much like a mummy—only slightly caved in. Clearly no corpse was inside. Even more amazing, the cloth which had covered Jesus' face lay by itself outside the sticky wrappings. Somehow the facial cloth had passed through the wrappings! They knew this was impossible, but there it was, right in front of their eyes. They were stunned.

Suddenly, two men stood beside them in the tomb, wearing white glowing garments. The women fell to the ground and shook with fear. "Why do you look for the living among the dead?" they asked. "He is not here; he has risen!" (Luke 24:5–6).

Today we celebrate this earth-changing, history-making, life-transforming event. The women left and told the disciples, who then told others, who told others. Thirty years later, Paul declared that the message of the resurrection "has been proclaimed to every creature under heaven" (Colossians 1:23). The greatest movement, with the greatest message, about the greatest Messiah the world has ever known continues to be proclaimed today.

Principle

The message of the resurrection is the greatest message in history.

Ponder

- When and how did you first encounter the message of the resurrection?
- How has it transformed your life?

Pursue: For a deeper dive, study Luke 24:1–8.

Lord Jesus, as you surprised those women on resurrection morning, thrill me once again with the joy of the empty tomb.

All Is Well

In March 1912, three members of Robert Scott's Antarctic expedition sat huddled in an ice hut, awaiting death. On perhaps the final day of his life, Dr. Edward Wilson wrote these words to his wife, "Don't be unhappy. . . . All is well. . . . We will all meet after death, and death has no terrors. . . . All the things I had hoped to do with you after this Expedition are as nothing now, but there are greater things for us in the world to come. . . . All is well."[11]

What would cause a man to pen the words "All is well" as he froze to death? Edward Wilson clung to an undeniable confidence that death would open the door to an unending new life. In contrast, Bertrand Russell, arguably the leading atheist of the twentieth century, in *A Free Man's Worship* wrote that the foundation of life itself is built upon "unyielding despair."[12]

Paul penned this haunting phrase: "We do not want you to be uninformed about those who sleep in death, so that you do not grieve like the rest of mankind, who have no hope" (1 Thessalonians 4:13). Imagine a life without hope—a life without Jesus. Our greatest hope would be eternal nothingness . . . grim, unyielding despair. It's too horrible to imagine.

But Jesus promises life after life to his followers. In his letter to the Corinthians, Paul declares, "Christ has been raised from the dead. He is the first of a great harvest of all who have died" (1 Corinthians 15:20 NLT). Then he adds, "When our dying bodies have been transformed into bodies that will never die, this Scripture will be fulfilled: 'Death is swallowed up in victory'" (v. 54 NLT).

In triumph, Paul declares. "But thank God! He gives us victory over sin and death through our Lord Jesus Christ" (v. 57 NLT). This is why followers of Jesus can live in unshakable hope. Through his resurrection, we share in his victory over death.

Quite a contrast to the "unyielding despair" of Bertrand Russell. Instead, like Edward Wilson, we cling to God's promise, knowing that in death we step into the most amazing life we could ever imagine.

We have the choice to immerse our hearts in hope rather than caving into despair. Hope in Jesus enables us to rise above our circumstances as we soar on a higher level and embrace the hope offered through the resurrection. Even in the worst situations life offers, we can say, "All is well."

Principle

Hope in Jesus enables us to say, "All is well."

Ponder

- What specific aspects of this world pull your attention away from Jesus and the hope he offers?
- How can you begin to focus more on this hope today?

Pursue: For a deeper dive, study 1 Corinthians 15:50–58.

Lord Jesus, thank you for the hope you offer even amid life's worst circumstances. I open my heart to you today to receive your gift of life and hope.

EPILOGUE

What the Resurrection Means to Me

I awoke in the night and listened for my wife's breathing, but I heard none. When I turned on the light, I discovered that Linda had departed this world.

Linda and I were married for fifty years before she withered away from ovarian cancer. During those months, words like *overwhelming*, *devastating*, *agonizing* passed through my lips as I cried out to God. But I never uttered the word *hopeless*. Because I'm not.

We use the expression "as silent as the tomb." But not so with the tomb of Jesus. It may have been quiet, but it was far from silent. When Jesus arose, that tomb screamed, like a divine megaphone, "There is hope beyond the grave!" And this reality changes everything.

The empty tomb stands as an eternal reminder that God will never abandon us. He says so in the book of Hebrews, "I will never [under any circumstances] desert you [nor give you up nor leave you without support, nor will I in any degree leave you helpless], nor will I forsake or let you down or relax My hold on you [assuredly not]!" (13:5 AMP). This is a pretty emphatic promise.

During the darkest night of the soul, our Saviour whispers, "I am with you, child." When our heart aches so badly we're afraid it might explode, he calms us with his peace that transcends understanding. When we think we can't survive another minute—and honestly, we don't really want to—he gives us the strength to continue living. When we bury our head in our pillow and sob so much that no more tears will flow, he weeps with us.

On some days this has been my story. But—I say it again—I have never felt hopeless or abandoned. I live in the certainty that I will see Linda again along with other dear friends who have entered not the land of the dead but the land of the living. They're experiencing more life than any of us on earth have ever known. With excitement, I anticipate great adventures ahead, shared with Linda and my friends. Nothing we've ever experienced could even remotely compare.

On the last night of her life, I sat by Linda's bed as her emaciated body clung to life. I held her hand and played songs we loved from our dating and early marriage years. I spoke of special memories and told her how deeply I loved her. Finally, I arose, kissed her forehead, and said, "Goodbye." But it wasn't really goodbye. It was "See you later." Because I will.

With unparalleled hope, I long for the day when I will pass through the portal into eternity. Linda will be there to greet me and say, "Hello," knowing that we'll never again say, "Goodbye." More than you can imagine, this hope sustains me. It gives me joy and strength—and a reason to live another day. Hope is no longer merely a word for me. It flows through my veins. This is what the resurrection means to me.

A FINAL WORD

Jesus told Nicodemus, "For God so loved the world that he gave his one and only Son, that whoever believes in him shall not perish but have eternal life" (John 3:16).

I hope these devotions have been a blessing to you and have reassured you or helped you believe that Jesus truly is who he claimed to be: God in human form. If you believe Jesus died for your sins and was raised from the dead, your next step is to declare your faith in him.

The apostle Paul told the Romans, "If you declare with your mouth, 'Jesus is Lord,' and believe in your heart that God raised him from the dead, you will be saved. For it is with your heart that you believe and are justified [restored to a right relationship with God] and it is with your mouth that you profess your faith and are saved" (Romans 10:9–10). Ask Jesus to forgive you and save you from your sins.

Then find a church that honours the Bible as God's Word and be baptised as a public declaration of the death, burial, and resurrection of Jesus (Romans 6:3–6). Your commitment will set you on a new path in life as a follower of Jesus. You can begin to experience eternal life right now and know the love, joy, and peace the risen Saviour offers each of us.

ABOUT THE AUTHOR

Barney Cargile and his wife, Linda, were married fifty years before she went home to be with Jesus. He lives on their small farm in Santa Rosa, California. He is a semi-retired pastor with Santa Rosa Christian Church who loves writing, travelling, and playing Monster with his grandkids. Barney travels the world, bringing hope and encouragement to those who need it most. He also works with the Redwood Gospel Mission and with The Ark, a recovery home, helping rescue those trapped in addiction, domestic violence, and human trafficking.

Barney is the author of the morning-and-evening devotional, *The Perfect Gift: Unwrapping True Joy for Christmas*, as well as *Thriving in Quarantine*, a number one bestseller on Amazon, and *Thriving in Troubled Times*. In addition, Barney has written several devotions for *The Upper Room*, a daily devotional read by over two million people in over one hundred countries, and has penned articles for *The Christian Journal* and his own blog, *Barney's Bullet*.

For information on Barney's future books or to subscribe to his weekly blog, please visit BarneyCargile.com or email him at barneyc3@gmail.com.

NOTES

Introduction

1. Ian Duncan, "40 Years Ago, a 737 Crashed into the 14th Street Bridge During a Snowstorm, Killing 78," *The Washington Post*, accessed February 21, 2024, https://www.washingtonpost.com /transportation/2022/01/13/air-florida-crash-40-years/.

Part One

1. Rick Reilly, "The Play of the Year," Vault, accessed May 4, 2024, https://vault.si.com/vault/2002/11/18/the-play-of-the -year.

2. "The Janitor Story from Crucial Accountability," YouTube, accessed February 21, 2024, https://www.youtube.com /watch?v=_DQYArmi5L0.

3. "Leonardo da Vinci Painting 'Salvator Mundi' Sold for Record $450.3 Million," Fox News, published November 15, 2017, updated November 16, 2017, https://www.foxnews.com/world /leonardo-da-vinci-painting-salvator-mundi-sold-for-record -450-3-million.

4. William H. Cook, *Success, Motivation, and the Scriptures* (Nashville: Baptist Sunday School Board, 1991), 91.

5. Andreana Lefton, "13 Odd Predictions about the Future That People in Past Decades Got Wrong—And Right," Bob Vila, February 7, 2019, https://www.bobvila.com/slideshow/13-odd -predictions-about-the-future-that-people-in-past-decades -got-wrong-and-right-52637.

6. "Did Jesus Fulfil Old Testament Prophecy?" Josh McDowell, A Cru Ministry, accessed April 29, 2024, https://www.josh.org /jesus-fulfil-prophecy/.

7. Josh McDowell, "The Probability of 8 Prophecies of 333 Fulfilled by Christ," Internet Archive, accessed April 1, 2024, https://archive.org/details/the-probability-of-8-prophecies-of -333-fulfilled-by-christ-by-josh-mc-dowell.

Part Two

1. Sir Thomas More, translated by Mary Gottschalk, *A Dialogueueueueueueueueue of Comfort Against Tribulation*, 3.14, 227.

2. C. S. Lewis, *Mere Christianity* (New York: MacMillan Paperbacks Edition, 1960), 56.

3. For more on the liar, lunatic, Lord concept, see Kyle Barton, "The History of the Liar, Lunatic, Lord Trilemma," Conversant Faith, May 4, 2012, https://conversantfaith.com/2012/05 /04/the-history-of-liar-lunatic-lord-trilemma/.

4. "Longest Time Breath Held Voluntarily Underwater (Male)," Guinness World Records, accessed February 21, 2024, https:// www.guinnessworldrecords.com/world-records/longest-time -breath-held-voluntarily-(male).

5. Madeline Levine, *The Price of Privilege: How Parental Pressure and Material Advantage Are Creating a Generation of Disconnected and Unhappy Kids* (New York: HarperCollins, 2006), 3.

6. "French Mayor Tells Locals Not to Die," Reuters, March 5, 2008, https://www.reuters.com/article/idUSL05520766/.

Part Three

1. "Insulas," That the World May Know, with Ray Vander Laan, accessed February 21, 2024, https://www.thattheworldmayknow .com/insulas.

2. H. R. Jerajani, Bhagyashri Jaju, M. M. Phiske, and Nitin Lade, "Hematohidrosis—A Rare Clinical Phenomenon," *Indian Journal of Dermatology* (July–September 2009): 290–292, accessed February 21, 2024, https://www.ncbi.nlm.nih.gov/pmc/articles/PMC2810702/#:~:text=Jesus%20Christ%20experienced%20hematohidrosis%20while,blood%20falling%20to%20the%20ground.%E2%80%9D

3. Rick Renner, "How Many Soldiers Does It Take to Arrest One Man?" Faith, accessed February 21, 2024, https://www.cfaith.com/index.php/blog/how-many-soldiers-does-it-take-to-arrest-one-man.

4. Robert Robinson, "Come Thou Fount of Every Blessing," lyrics penned in 1758.

5. "The Story of Shep," Fort Benton, accessed February 21, 2024, http://www.fortbenton.com/shep.html.

6. "Two Arrested in Brawl over Prize Tickets at Chuck E. Cheese," CBS News, October 21, 2013, https://www.cbsnews.com/chicago/news/two-arrested-in-brawl-over-prize-tickets-at-chuck-e-cheese/.

7. Fleming Rutledge, *The Undoing of Death* (Grand Rapids, MI: Wm. B. Eerdmans Publishing Co., 2002), 117–18.

Part Four

1. John Stott, *The Cross of Christ*, 20th anniversary edition (Westmont, IL: IVP Books, 2006), 85.

2. Anthony Robbins, *Unlimited Power* (New York: Ballantine Books, 1986), 184–85.

3. M. Tullius Cicero, *Speech before Roman Citizens on Behalf of Gaius Rabirius, Defendant Against the Charge of Treason*, ed. William Blake Tyrrell, 5.16, http://data.perseus.org/citations/urn:cts:latinLit:phi0474.phi012.perseus-eng2:5.16.

4. "50-Year Grudge Leads to S.D. Killing, Life Prison Term," CBSnews.com, accessed April 30, 2024, https://www.cbsnews.com/news/50-year-grudge-leads-to-sd-killing-life-prison-term/.

5. "11 Famous Last Words, Featuring Oscar Wilde and Leonard Nimoy," Marie Curie, March 16, 2017, https://www.mariecurie.org.uk/talkabout/articles/11-famous-last-words-oscar-wilde-leonard-nimoy/152953.

6. Micheal Maynard, "It Is Finished . . . The Last Words of Jesus," SweetWaterNow, June 25, 2017, https://www.sweetwaternow.com/it-is-finished-the-last-words-of-jesus/.

7. Maynard, "It Is Finished."

8. "John F. Kennedy Jnr. under the Resolute Desk," Iconic Photos, September 3, 2010, https://iconicphotos.wordpress.com/2010/09/03/john-f-kennedy-jnr-under-the-resolute-desk/.

9. Alfred Edersheim, *The Life and Times of Jesus the Messiah*, vol. 2 (London: Longman's, Green, and Co., 1883), 609, https://books.google.com/books?id=VJUHAAAAQAAJ.

10. "Headless Snake Points to Satan's Demise," PreachingToday, accessed April 1, 2024, https://www.preachingtoday.com/illustrations/2011/april/7041111.html.

11. "Inky the Octopus Escapes from a New Zealand Aquarium," The New York Times, April 14, 2014, https://www.nytimes.com/2016/04/14/world/asia/inky-octopus-new-zealand-aquarium.html.

12. Henry Gariepy, *40 Days with the Saviour: Preparing Your Heart for Easter* (Nashville: Thomas Nelson Publishers, 1995), xiii–xiv.

13. Randy Alcorn, "Peace Child Revisited, 50 Years after First Contact," Eternal Perspective Ministries, May 3, 2013, https://www.epm.org/blog/2013/May/3/peace-child.

14. Robert L. Odom, ed., "Jewish Division of Days into Hours," Ministry Magazine, accessed February 21, 2024, https://www.ministrymagazine.org/archive/1946/04/jewish-division-of-day-into-hours#:~:text=%22Peter%20and%20John%20went%20up,o'clock%20in%20the%20afternoon.

15. Eric Pfeiffer, "Man Allegedly Steals $100K Coin Collection, Then Spends at Face Value on Pizza and a Movie," Yahoo! News, September 21, 2012, https://news.yahoo.com/blogs /sideshow/man-allegedly-steals-100k-coin-collection-then -spends-214047054.html.

Part Five

1. Martin E. Marty, "Professor Pelikan: A keen sense of what matters," *The Christian Century*, June 13, 2006, https://www .christiancentury.org/article/2006-06/professor-pelikan.

2. C. S. Lewis, *Miracles* (New York: Touchstone, 1996), 188–91.

3. *The Guinness Book of World Records* (New York: Bantam, 1990), 211.

4. Adapted from a sermon by Lee Strobel, "Jesus Is Alive—True or False," Sermon Central, September 26, 2004, https://www .sermoncentral.com/sermons/jesus-is-alive-true-or-false-lee -strobel-sermon-on-apologetics-jesus-72274.

5. Jerry Fenter, "The Most Excellent Way: Love Matters," Sermons.Logos, accessed February 21, 2024, https://sermons .faithlife.com/sermons/62724-the-most-excellent-way:-love -matters.

6. Anna Slater, "Family Dog Found 'Dead' Digs His Way Out of His Grave and Returns to Owners," Mirror, October 8, 2023, https://www.mirror.co.uk/news/world-news/family-dog-found -dead-digs-31093185.

7. "Woman Discovers She's Dead," IOL, January 9, 2007, https:// www.iol.co.za/news/eish/woman-discovers-shes-dead-310210.

8. Doron Nof, Ian McKeague, and Nathan Paldor, "Is There a Paleolimnological Explanation for 'Walking on Water' in the Sea of Galilee?" *Journal of Paleolimnology* 35 (2006): 417–39, https://doi.org/10.1007/s10933-005-1996-1.

9. "James J. Braddock," Britannica, accessed February 21, 2024, https://www.britannica.com/biography/James-J-Braddock.

10. Lou Nicholes, "Barnhouse: The Shadow of Death," *Family Times*, accessed February 21, 2024, https://www.family-times .net/illustration/Troubled/200318/.

11. Ann Berghaus, "The Hiller Family," ed. by Carolyn Harris, Wilmington Memorial Library, accessed February 21, 2024, https://wilmlibrary.org/community/local-history/articles -events/hiller/#house.

12. "Shopper Tries to Pass a $1 Million Dollar Bill," CBSNews .com, October 9, 2007, https://www.cbsnews.com/news /shopper-tries-to-pass-a-1-million-bill/.

13. Alex Bilmes, "Paul McCartney: The Esquire Interview," Esquire, updated June 20, 2022, https://www.esquire.com/uk /culture/a8511/paul-mccartney-interview/.

14. David Dye, "Paul McCartney: An Icon Ages Gracefully," National Public Radio, December 31, 2007, https://www.npr .org/2007/12/31/11781240/paul-mccartney-an-icon-ages -gracefully.

15. Brad Bloom, "Paul Anderson—Build Something Bigger Than Record-Setting Strength," Faith and Fitness Magazine, Faithandfitness.net, August 9, 2023, https://faithandfitness.net /paul-anderson-build-something-bigger-than-record-setting -strength/.

Part Six

1. Frederica Matthewes-Green, *Bread and Wine: Readings for Lent and Easter* (Maryknoll, NY: Orbis Books, 2005), 267.

2. Paul Sexton, "'Garden Party': The Reinvention of Rick Nelson," UDiscoverMusic, December 9, 2023, https://www .udiscovermusic.com/stories/rick-nelson-garden-party-song /#:~:text=The%20lyric%20was%20a%20real,Bo%20 Diddley%2C%20and%20Bobby%20Rydell.

3. R. Tamasy, "A Solution Better Than Butting," CBMC International, January 21, 2013, https://www.cbmcint.com/a-solution -better-than-butting-heads/.

4. The Associated Press, "Cranky Man Shoots Lawn Mower for Not Starting," NBC News, July 25, 2008, https://www.nbcnews.com/id/wbna25854715.

5. "Trashing the Temple Courts: What Was That All About?" Honest about My Faith, March 30, 2015, https://honestaboutmyfaith.wordpress.com/2015/03/30/trashing-the-temple-courts-what-was-that-all-about/.

6. Walt Hickey, "Northern Ireland Installed Hilarious Fake Storefronts to Cover Up Its Crappy Abandoned Buildings before the G8 Summit," Business Insider, June 4, 2013, https://www.businessinsider.com/here-are-the-hilarious-fake-storefronts-northern-ireland-installed-to-hide-crappy-buildings-ahead-of-the-g8-summit-2013-6.

7. Bob Mims, "Utah Duck Hunter Shot in Buttocks by His Dog," *Salt Lake Tribune*, November 30, 2011, https://archive.sltrib.com/article.php?id=53020150&itype=CMSID.

8. Adapted from Brennan Manning, *The Ragamuffin Gospel: Good News for the Bedraggled, Beat-Up, and Burnt Out* (Sisters, OR: Multnomah, 2008), 104.

9. Steve Shepherd, *The Cross of Christ*, Sermon Central, February 27, 2004, https://www.sermoncentral.com/sermons/the-cross-of-christ-steve-shepherd-sermon-on-cross-66260.

10. All three quotations from Chris Altrock, *The Cross: Saved by the Shame of It All* (Joplin, MO: College Press Publishing Company, 1998), 117, 26, 43.

11. "Edward Wilson's Penultimate Letter to His Wife, Oriana," The Cheltenham Trust, accessed February 27, 2024, https://www.cheltenhammuseum.org.uk/collection/edward-wilsons-last-letter-to-his-wife-oriana/.

12. Bertrand Russell, "A Free Man's Worship," University of Notre Dame, accessed March 22, 2024, https://www3.nd.edu/~afreddos/courses/264/fmw.htm.

Spread the Word
by Doing One Thing.

- Give a copy of this book as a gift.

- Share the QR code link via your social media.

- Write a review of this book on your blog, favorite bookseller's website, or at ODB.org/store.

- Recommend this book to your church, small group, or book club.

Connect with us. ⓕ ⓘ

Our Daily Bread Publishing
PO Box 3566, Grand Rapids, MI 49501, USA
Email: books@odb.org

Love God. Love Others.

with  Our Daily Bread.

Your gift changes lives.

Connect with us. ⨍ ⃝

Our Daily Bread Publishing
PO Box 3566, Grand Rapids, MI 49501, USA
Email: books@odb.org